What does it feel like in space?
How long does it take to get used to space?
Do you look the same in space?
Does your hair float out from your head?
What kind of work did you do on Skylab?
Was it hard to work while in a space suit?
How did you drink?
How did you bathe?

All the answers to all the questions you have about living in space, including the question most often asked . . .

HOW DO YOU GO TO THE BATHROOM IN SPACE?

WILLIAM R. POGUE, ASTRONAUT

HOW DO YOU GO TO THE BATHROOM IN SPACE?

A TOM DOHERTY ASSOCIATES BOOK

1. How old are you?

I was born in 1930. I was forty-three years old when our mission launched to visit Skylab and I celebrated my forty-fourth birthday while in space.

2. What is your academic background?

I have a Bachelor of Science degree in secondary education and a Master of Science degree in mathematics, and I taught undergraduate mathematics at the Air Force Academy.

3. Are you a graduate of a service academy?

No, I attended a civilian college and received my commission through the Air Force aviation cadet program during the Korean conflict.

4. Which branch of the military (service) were you in? How long?

I was in the Air Force for twenty-five years, nine of which were spent with NASA as an astronaut.

5. What kind of airplanes have you flown?

Over fifty types and models of American and British aircraft, mostly fighter aircraft.

6. What kind of airplane did you fly in Korea?

The F-84G, a fighter-bomber.

7. When did you fly with the Thunderbirds? What airplane did you fly with the aerobatic team? What position?

I flew with the Thunderbirds, the Air Force aerobatic team, from 1955 to 1957. I flew as solo pilot in the F-84F and F-100C, and for over a year, also in the F-100C, I was slot pilot in the diamond formation.

8. Which do you think was riskier, flying with the Thunderbirds or going into space?

Flying with the Thunderbirds was probably riskier, but I never thought of it as being dangerous. The most hazardous flying I ever did was instructing students in aerial gunnery training.

9. Which group of astronauts were you in? When were you selected to be an astronaut? When did you leave the space program?

I was in the fifth group of astronauts selected in 1966 and left the space program in September, 1977. I wanted to become an astronaut because it seemed to be the highest goal attainable for a pilot as well as being interesting and exciting work.

10. What were the names of the other men on your mission?

Colonel Gerald (Jerry) P. Carr, a Marine Corps fighter pilot, was the Commander and Dr. Edward (Ed) G. Gibson was the Scientist Pilot.

11. What do you think was Skylab's greatest contribution?

The greatest immediate contribution was the demonstration of man's ability to live and work in weightlessness for long periods (up to three months). The studies of the Earth and sun provided information for long-term investigations, and their full contribution may not be known for many years.

12. Aren't you really thrown back at liftoff? (There is a widespread belief that the astronauts feel their strongest force effect from the engine thrust at the time of liftoff.)

The force on the astronaut at liftoff isn't as great as commonly believed. In the older Saturn boosters, the astronauts were pressed back in the couches at just a bit more than their normal body weight; an astronaut weighing 150 pounds, for instance, would feel like he weighed 165 pounds. On the Space Shuttle, the same astronaut would be pressed back into the seat with a force of about 225 pounds. This is much higher liftoff acceleration than felt on the older boosters, but it isn't nearly the force felt later on during boost. On Saturn boosters (rockets), the astronauts felt the most force just as the first stage of the rocket had burned up most of its fuel—about four times heavier than normal. The Space Shuttle thrust is controlled so that the most force the astronauts feel is about three times their normal weight.

13. What does it feel like in space?

The first thing you notice when you go into space is an absence of pressure on your body. You may feel lightheaded or giddy. After a half-hour or so, your face may feel flushed and you might feel a throbbing in your neck. As you move about, you will notice a strong sensation of spinning or tumbling every time you turn or nod your head. This makes some people uncomfortable or nauseated. You will also have a very "full feeling" or stuffiness in your head. You may get a bad headache after a few hours, and this too may make you feel sick at your stomach.

Most all of these symptoms will go away in a few days. The head congestion or stuffiness may bother you off and on during your entire time in space. Throughout the space flight, you will feel a powerful sensation of tumbling or spinning every time you move your head too fast.

There are two things you can do on Earth to get a reasonable idea what it feels like in space. The general floating feeling is quite similar to the effect of relaxing in a swimming pool. The head stuffiness experienced in space is much like the uncomfortable feeling that one gets when hanging upside-down from gymnast bars. Normally, it is uncomfortable to stay in this position beyond a minute or two because of the full feeling in the head caused by the upside-down position.

14. How long does it take to get used to space?

It takes the body about three days to adjust to the weightlessness. You will become accustomed to working in space in a few hours, but you will be learning better ways to do things throughout the mission. Even though I got sick the first evening in space, the following day, which was our first full day in orbit, I worked fourteen hours.

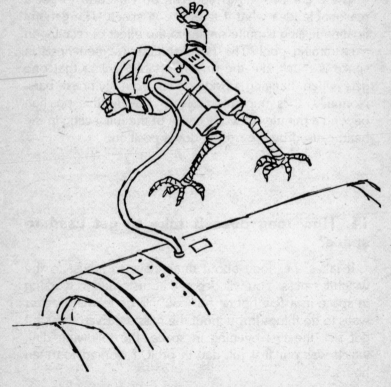

BIRDLEGS

15. When sailors go to sea, they gradually get their "sea legs." Did you get "space legs" after being in space for a while?

We did, quite literally, develop space legs. We called it "bird legs," because our legs became thinner and thinner as the weeks passed. The calves, in particular, became quite small. During the first few days in space, the legs become smaller because the muscles of the legs force blood and other fluids toward the upper part of the body, thus decreasing the girth measurement around the thighs and calves. In addition, muscle tissue is progressively lost due to insufficient exercise. These changes produce a "bird leg" effect.

16. What happened to your body in space?

We grew 1½ to 2¼ inches taller. This height increase was due to spinal lengthening and straightening. The discs between the vertebrae expand and compress slightly, depending on the weight the back is supporting. Even on Earth, an adult will be slightly taller (about one half-inch) in the morning than in the evening because the discs expand during sleep and compress as you walk or sit during the day. In weightlessness, the discs expand, but they don't compress again, because there is never weight on the spine. Our space suits were custom-tailored on Earth to our height and posture, thus, they fit tighter in space because of the height increase. Also, my waist measurement decreased by almost three inches, due to an upward shift of the internal organs in the body creating a "wasp waist" appearance.

In addition to the height increase and waist thinning,

WE GREW TALLER

the posture changes slightly. Your relaxed body posture is semi-erect with the knees slightly bent, head raised or tilted backward, shoulders up (similar to a "shrug" gesture), and arms floating up and forward with your hands about chest height. Because of the raised position of the arms, it was an effort to work at waist height as you ordinarily do; you must continually force your arms down to waist level to do work on surfaces at "table height."

Also, you can't remain in a seated position without a belt to hold your body down in the seat. The body's tendency to resume the erect posture is quite hard to oppose by using the abdominal muscles. It's also very hard to bend forward. We found it much easier to pull our legs upward to lace our shoes rather than to bend down. Inability to bend forward easily also made it harder to get the upper part of the one-piece space suits over our heads. We had to duck our heads down and lift the top half of the suits up to get our heads through the neck ring.

17. Do you look the same in space?

No, facial appearance changes quite a lot. I was really surprised, if not shocked, the first time I looked in the mirror; I didn't look like me anymore. Loose flesh on the face rises, or floats, on the bone structure, giving a high-cheekboned or Oriental appearance. The face also looks a bit puffy, with bags under the eyes, especially during the first few days, and the veins in your forehead and neck appear swollen. After about three or four days,

BEFORE   DURING   AFTER

some of the facial puffiness (edema) and vein enlarge-
ment goes away, but your face still looks quite a bit
different.

18. Did you gain or lose weight?

We lost about three or four pounds during the first
four days of the mission. Then we gradually regained
most of the loss, so that, by the end of the mission, we
were just about back to our weight at launch.

Most of the early flight weight loss is caused by
elimination (reduction) of body fluids. The fluid shift
causes excessive fluids in the upper torso; the body
senses this localized excess and reduces the total body
fluid level through urination.

19. If you were weightless, how could you weigh yourself?

We really didn't weigh ourselves the same way we
did on Earth because a spring or balance scale wouldn't
work. However, we could determine body mass, and
then convert this to an equivalent Earth weight, by
sitting in a special chair that swung back and forth on
springs. The time it took for each swing of the chair was
measured and used by a computer to determine our
body mass, or Earth weight. This device was called a
Body Mass Measurement Device (BMMD).

I found the device mildly unpleasant because the

LIVE AND WORK IN
WEIGHTLESSNESS

metal was cold and we used it the first thing after waking up, while we were still in our underwear. The chair was actually more like a box, and we had to get in it with our knees doubled up under our chin. This jammed-up posture was required to reduce fluid slosh and internal organ movement in our bodies during the oscillations of the chair. This peculiar posture was necessary to get an accurate reading with the device.

20. Is it true that you lost a lot of calcium from your bones and that this may make long missions impossible?

This is partly correct. We did lose calcium from the bones, but it wasn't excessive. After Skylab, NASA doctors were worried that this loss might become bad enough on long space flights to cause serious harm to the skeletons of astronauts. Since then, the Russians have completed three space missions of six months each. They have indicated that the rate of calcium loss slows significantly or stops after four or five months. If this is correct, then calcium loss, which is similar to osteoporosis and also called bone mass loss or bone demineralization, will not limit the length of time people can stay in weightlessness. It appears that the calcium loss is similar to that experienced by bedrest patients on Earth. Such patients show a marked decrease in the rate of calcium loss after the first few months of being bedridden.

I have had no ill effects from this. Incidentally, the bone mass loss can not be balanced by taking mineral supplements. Mineral supplements are not used by the body to replace losses in the bones and can contribute to the development of kidney stones.

21. Do you get tired in space?

Yes, we did get tired in weightlessness. Heavy exercise left us with a comfortable tired feeling. We also experienced a psychological weariness from rushing and from mental pressure to keep on schedule. All astronauts on Skylab have reported a sort of overall tiredness, a fatigue or run-down feeling, that often occurred about three or four hours after eating. I called it "space crud." It's sort of like the down-and-out feeling you have when you're coming down with a bad cold or the flu. I still don't understand what caused this, but we learned very quickly that it was unwise to skip meals to save time. If we did, we would begin to feel bad and were much more likely to make a mistake.

I noticed one peculiar inconsistency about the space crud; I didn't develop it on space walks, even though I went for six to seven hours without eating or drinking. I don't know why the effects should be absent on space walks, unless it was because we enjoyed it so much that it helped to offset the occurrence of the symptoms.

22. Does your hair float out from your head?

Our hair was short enough that this wasn't a problem. But women astronauts might have a problem with this. It's so easy to get things snagged and tangled up in weightlessness that I wouldn't be surprised if women or men with long hair have to wear a hair covering to avoid a problem. Sally Ride, America's first woman in space, trimmed and curled her hair before flight. Based on her experience she feels that long hair would be difficult to manage in weightlessness.

Onboard movie photos taken on the Twelfth shuttle flight (mission 41D) show astronaut Judy Resnik's hairdo puffed and raised in back. In one scene her hair appears to cause another crewmember problems when they both try to use the same window to observe a satellite deployment.

23. How did you breathe? Was breathing any different?

The spacecraft is pressurized or filled with air; on Skylab space walks the space suit was inflated by a steady flow of air supplied through a long hose called an umbilical. The continuous flow made sure there was always fresh air in the suit. Suits used by Shuttle astronauts contain an oxygen supply in tanks attached to the back of the suit and the astronauts are not attached to the Shuttle by a hose or an umbilical.

Although we didn't notice any difference, tests made on Skylab showed we couldn't breathe as deeply. In weightlessness, there is a noticeable shift of the abdominal organs upward toward the rib cage. Apparently, this appears to be the main reason it was harder to take deep breaths.

24. How did you avoid high humidity from building up, due to respiration and evaporation from the body, in the air?

The air inside Skylab was circulated across cold metal surfaces where water vapor condensed and was then collected and transferred into a waste water tank. The atmosphere inside was usually quite dry.

25. What kind of soap did you use?

We used both bar and liquid soap (shampoo). It was similar to Neutragena. The bar soap had a slab of iron imbedded in it so it would stick to the magnetized surfaces in the bathroom.

26. What is warp (space warp)?

Space warp is the imaginary concept of science fiction writers. It is envisioned as a way of getting from one place to another without crossing the distance between them. At the present time, no one is able to achieve such a thing as space warp.

27. How did you get from one place to another?

In Skylab, we pulled ourselves along structural surfaces by using handholds (special hand grips or handles) or other parts of the spacecraft; we also shoved or pushed off from one position to float to the next location. When shoving off to float across a large empty volume, we went headfirst, feet-first, and also sideways—launching ourselves in a manner to keep from tumbling en route. We were usually able to arrive at the next location in the best position to grasp and hold fixtures. In small volumes, however, we had to be careful to avoid damage to the spacecraft when we moved around. Headfirst motion was the one used most often.

On space walks, transfer handholds were essential in getting from one position to the next. Foot restraints were located at all *planned* work stations so that the astronaut didn't have to hold on to something continuously in order to maintain his position. Transfer handholds were often similar to the rungs of a ladder and were spaced for moving hand-over-hand to travel between locations.

The term "space walk" is a popular name for what we called Extra Vehicular Activity or EVA. I tried to walk across a grid mesh surface by using a special pair of "mushrooms" I attached to the bottom of my shoes in place of the metal triangular cleats. Every time I stretched out my foot to take the next step, my foot just floated in the air and I had to exert effort to bend forward to get my foot down on the surface. It required a lot of extra work, so I took the mushrooms off and never used them again.

Space Shuttle astronauts also use handholds on space walks. On some flights, they will use a Manned Maneuvering Unit (MMU) which is actually a miniature spacecraft that can be flown free of the Shuttle Orbiter. The MMU will greatly increase the work capability of astronauts on space walks.

28. What kind of work did you do on Skylab?

We operated equipment and instruments for more than fifty experiments. The three principal experiments were performed throughout the mission and occupied a lot of time each day. We had a solar observatory for making observations of the sun, cameras and other instruments for studying the Earth, and equipment for several medical experiments to determine the long-term effects of weightlessness.

29. Was it hard work?

Some work tasks were very difficult, but most were routine and merely took adequate time. The hardest jobs were repair and maintenance tasks that involved a lot of physical force, such as pushing, pulling, or twisting.

Sometimes there was no convenient surface or hand-grip to hold on to with the free hand, so as to balance the force applied with the working hand. A typical problem we faced was in trying to loosen or tighten screws on a large flat surface. To apply a strong twist force, you normally have to push on the screwdriver while twisting it. In doing one repair job, I found it necessary to rig pull straps for my left hand so I could pull to balance the push force of my right hand. If you're patient and aren't pressed for time, these problems become an interesting challenge. If you're trying to meet a critical time schedule, it can be very irritating and frustrating.

On the average, we figured it took about twice the time to do a job in weightlessness than it took on Earth. One particular servicing task I did was extremely hard to do even on the ground. It involved reaching into an enclosed area to disconnect and reconnect two plumbing lines by sliding metal sleeves on pipes that ran sideways to my arm direction. I only had to do it once in space, but that was enough. My legs were thrashing around as I tried to get my arms in the best position, and, when I finally finished, my wrists were scratched

WE DIDN'T HAVE THE RIGHT TOOLS

and cut from banging into the sheet-metal edges around the access opening. I really felt "pooped" by the end of the day. You can't "stretch yourself" like you can on Earth when you keep going to finish a long job.

30. What did you do on space walks?

On space walks, we repaired a radar antenna used for Earth studies and a telescope used to look at the sun. On the inside of Skylab, we repaired cooling systems, tape recorders, and many of the scientific instruments.

Some of the repair jobs were really crude because we didn't have the right tools or materials. Ed Gibson operated one instrument that used batteries to power a light inside to create a sighting reference on a mirror surface. The batteries kept running down and Ed had to keep installing fresh batteries. Finally, he ran out of spare batteries, so he had to dig out some other batteries, which were intended for our tape recorders, and try to make them work. They didn't fit in the instrument, so he had to run wires from the inside of the instrument and tape them on the battery terminals. It worked, but it really looked weird. The clump of batteries sort of floated on the end of the wires, and Ed finally had to tape the whole glob on the side of the instrument. Ed said we were bumping into the batteries and loosening the wires. I was surprised that the tape held the wires snuggly enough against the battery terminals to make a good electrical connection. Early in Skylab training we had asked for a soldering iron as a part of our tool kit, but the mission planners said there was no need for one and disapproved the request. As it turned out, a soldering iron would have been very useful when Ed rigged his battery assembly.

31. Was it hard to work while in a space suit?

Yes. The suit is bulky and stiff, which makes it difficult to bend or turn your body. The gloves are very thick, so you don't have much feel. Because air pressure in the gloves tends to hold the fingers out straight, it is very tiring to maintain a grip on anything. I always felt like a "bull in a china closet" when working in a space suit. After doing a lot of work in a suit, my fingertips became very sore and tender and I had cuts and burns on my shoulders from the braided metal arm support cables inside the suit. Even so, we enjoyed the space walks and looked forward to the chance to get outside. I was out on a space walk once for six and a half hours and once for seven hours.

The suits used by Space Shuttle astronauts provide better torso mobility (twisting at the waist), the arms and legs are a bit easier to move and the suit is easier to put on. However, hand and finger movements still require a lot of effort and hand fatigue and finger irritation are still experienced.

32. When you were on a space walk, did you work during darkness? (The periods of light and dark are about fifty minutes and forty minutes respectively.)

Yes, if we had lights in the area where we were working. For some of the repair work there was no lighting provided, so we had to stop work while we were on the night side of the Earth. It can often cause difficulties when darkness comes right in the middle of a task.

33. What did you do if your nose itched when you were in your space suit?

Not only did my nose itch occasionally, but also my ears. Because a scratch is almost an involuntary reaction, I frequently reached up to scratch my nose and hit my helmet—which can make you feel really dumb. I scratched my nose by rubbing it on a little nose pincher device we used to clear our ears. If our ears stopped up or became uncomfortable due to pressure changes in the suit, the procedure was to press the nose against this open "V" device in order to hold our nostrils closed while we exerted a slight blowing pressure. This is a common technique used by fliers to clear their ears. This little nose pincher also made a nice nose scratcher. If our ears itched, we just had to tolerate it. I usually tried rubbing the side of my head against the inside of the helmet, but it didn't help much. The best thing to do was to think of something else.

34. Was it quiet or noisy in space?

Sound can't travel through space because there is no air to carry the sound waves. However, there was a moderate noise level inside Skylab, most of which was caused by pumps, fans, and voice chatter on the radio. We had a teleprinter which made a pecking sound similar to a typewriter—this made it difficult to sleep at times. Occasionally, small thrusters on the outside of Skylab would fire, which sounded like someone hammering on a large piece of metal. The most peculiar sound we noticed was a deep rumble which occurred about every forty-five minutes. It sounded like the roll of distant thunder. We finally decided it was due to alternate heating and cooling of the side of Skylab that faced the sun. This surface expanded as it heated up and shrank (contracted) as it cooled. The noise created was similar to the crackling sound made by a furnace or wood stove as it heats up or cools down. The total structure of Skylab was so large that it produced a low-pitched rumble instead of a crackling noise.

35. What kind of tools did you have?

Because of the long missions scheduled on Skylab, it was thought that we would need an assortment of tools to repair breakdowns in equipment. We had a rather complete set of light tools, and we used most of them at one time or the other. Most of the tools were bought at hardware stores, but some were specially made for anticipated repair work. The tools included various types of screwdrivers and pliers, socket wrenches, and torque wrenches. Special tool kits were also provided for repair

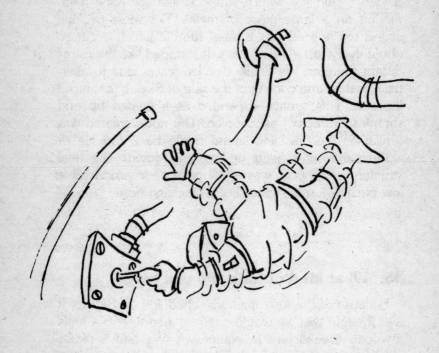

THE SCREW WOULDN'T TURN —
YOU WOULD

jobs on space walks. Each astronaut had pockets in his trousers to carry a Swiss army knife and a pair of surgical scissors, which were used frequently for minor repair work.

When using tools requiring a lot of force like screwdrivers or socket wrenches, it was necessary to have your body firmly restrained or tied down before applying force; otherwise, when you applied force, your body would move instead of the wrench. For example, if you floated over to a panel, inserted a screwdriver into the slot of a screw, and twisted your wrist, the screw wouldn't turn—you would!

36. Did you ever lose anything?

Yes. Several items were lost and never found. Frequently, our tableware, usually a knife, would get knocked off the magnetized surface on our food trays. The air flow in Skylab would usually carry the items to a filter screen in the air duct system, where they would stick due to the slight vacuum. This was the first place we looked when something was missing.

One day, when I whirled around to get a camera to take a picture of Hawaii, my eyeglasses flew off. I heard them bouncing around through the experiment compartment as I was taking the picture, but when I went to get them, I couldn't find them. Three days later, Dr. Gibson found them floating near the ceiling in his sleep compartment.

I had a spare set of half-specs, granny glasses, which I used until Ed found my bifocals. I didn't like the half-specs because the straight ear pieces allowed the lenses to float up off my nose and bob up and down in front of my eyes. It was very distracting when I was using both hands to do a job.

37. How did you clean the spacecraft, or did you have to clean the spacecraft?

As on Earth, a lot of trash accumulated during the day, but most of it was immediately placed in a waste container. However, bits of skin, fingernails, hair, food crumbs, odd pieces of paper, and the like tended to drift around and eventually were sucked up against air filters. We used vacuum cleaners to clean off the filters, and that took care of most of the problem. The worst mess was in the area where we ate. Small drops of liquid from our drinks and crumbs from our food would float around until they stuck on the wall or in an open grid ceiling above our food table, and it became quite dirty. Although we could see into this ceiling area, we couldn't get our hands in to wipe it clean, so it became progressively worse throughout the mission. Near the end of the flight, it began to look like the bottom of a bird cage. I just stopped looking at the ceiling after a while because it was such a mess.

38. How did you write?

I found that a lot of writing became an irritating task in weightlessness, particularly when it had to be done on narrow strips of paper that came out of our teleprinter.

This paper was just a bit wider than the paper used in cash registers. It tended to curl up and was hard to hold steady on a flat surface. We often used the food tray tops, our dinner table, as a desk, and we had to exert effort to bend forward to get into a good position to write. Also, we had to hold downward force to keep our hand and arms down on the table while writing. Other astronauts didn't seem to mind this as much as I did.

39. Did you use pen or pencil?

We used mechanical pencils, pressurized ball-point pens that assured ink flow in weightlessness, and felt-tip pens. The ball-points and mechanical pencils worked well, but felt-tips dried out very quickly in the low humidity of Skylab, so they weren't of much use.

Pencil leads did break off, but they didn't cause any problems, even though it would have been possible to get a piece in the eye—or inhale it.

40. How did you keep a book open to the right page?

This occasionally became a real problem. Most of our flight documents were printed on stiff paper and held together by metal rings which could be opened to insert or remove pages. We had clips to hold the books open to the right page, but they didn't attach very tightly and occasionally they would pop off and the whole book would fan open—costing us considerable time in relocating the right page. The covers were made of extra heavy paper to make it easy to find the front of the book and the index.

When reading a book from our personal library, which was mostly paperbacks, we held the book with one hand, with our thumb in the open crease, and dog-eared the pages to mark our place.

41. What would happen to water on Skylab? How did free water behave in weightlessness?

In weightlessness, water and other thin liquids must be fully enclosed in a container to prevent them from spilling and floating around. Water in a drinking glass would tend to crawl up the inside surface, over the edge, and down the outside of the glass. Free water droplets become spherical or ball-shaped. Large drops or balls of water quiver and jiggle like gelatin as they float about. On Skylab, we performed many science demonstrations with water drops.

42. Did you bring food, clothes, etc. with you when you went to visit Skylab?

We brought a twenty-eight day supply of food (food bars, some freeze-dried foods—and drinks) to supplement the fifty-six day supply already on board Skylab, and we brought enough underwear and socks for the extra month.

Each astronaut selected his menu items from a shop-

WATER IN A DRINKING GLASS
WOULD TEND TO CRAWL UP

ping list prepared by NASA dieticians. We had dehydrated scrambled eggs. After adding water and heating them, they were quite good. We had canned fruit (peaches, pears) and dried fruit (apricots). For the first time in space, we had frozen food, which included steak, prime rib, pork, and ice cream. We had no bread or milk. We also had a wide variety of drinks, which included orange, grapefruit, strawberry, cherry, grape, and coffee and tea.

The only food that was a disappointment was the chili. I was really looking forward to having it, but the oil separated from the meat and sauce and it looked very unappetizing when we opened the can. I stirred it up as much as I could and jammed my crackers into the can before eating it.

43. How did you keep frozen food frozen?

There was a food freezer on Skylab, which was kept below freezing by coolant chilled in a radiator on the outside at the rear of the space station. We had the same problem with frost inside the freezer as you have here on Earth, and we had to remove the frost frequently. We used wet cloths to melt the ice around the door and on the inside. It was a slow, unpleasant job, and we usually took turns during the process because our hands got so cold.

44. How did you cook your food?

We didn't cook our food, but we did warm solid foods like precooked meats and vegetables in their metal containers by placing them in food tray cavities that were warmed by electrical heating elements.

Skylab had a hot water system, and coffee or tea could be prepared easily and quickly.

45. How do you keep the food on your plate?

We didn't have plates. Our food came in cans and plastic bags that fitted into cavities in our food trays. We used a fork and spoon to get the food from the containers and a knife and fork to cut the solid meats.

There was a thin plastic cover over most of the canned food. We cut a crisscross slit in the plastic and fished the food out with a spoon or fork. The natural "stickiness" (surface tension) of the food and the plastic cover held it in quite well. Occasionally, little bits of food or meat juice would float out as we took a bite. We would dab at it with a tissue as it floated above the table, and we got most of it. Unfortunately, we didn't get it all, and the droplets would usually float up, due to airflow, and stick to the ceiling. Thick soups and ice cream tended to stick to the spoon, so you could eat them normally, as long as you didn't make any abrupt movements.

46. Did you have catsup and mustard?

Yes. It was in little plastic sacks similar to the kind you use at a fast-food restaurant. We also had hot sauce, liquid pepper in restaurant-type squeeze bottles, and horseradish, which we mixed into a paste and spread on our meat. The liquid pepper was especially good and had a full, fresh flavor.

We had salt water in a dispenser that looked like a hypodermic syringe with a plastic nozzle. We squirted the salt solution directly on our food.

NOTE: The first Skylab crew had no condiments at all. The Commander, Pete Conrad, really blasted the planners when he got back and raised such a fuss about the bland, yucky-tasting food that condiments were finally added. The second crew tried regular ground pepper and salt, but they didn't work too well. By the time we launched, the dietician had worked out a good scheme for dispensing a wide selection of condiments. Pete Conrad really did us a great service by insisting on the addition of condiments.

47. Did you have recycled water?

No. Skylab carried about one-thousand gallons of water for drinking and also for bathing. If Skylab had been designed for repeated visits over several years, then recycling of water would have been practical. The simplest recycling system is to remove water from the spacecraft atmosphere. This water would come from exhaled air and moisture evaporated from the skin, i.e. sweat. We actually removed this water, but we didn't use it for anything. It was collected in a waste water tank. (The Russian cosmonauts reuse this water in their Salyut space station.) A more complete water recycling scheme would also include reprocessing of liquid body waste, urine.

If this sounds offensive, just remember that the Earth is a closed life (ecological) system. Something has to happen to all the liquid waste of animal life. It is recycled in our natural system through evaporation and subsequent rainfall, if you're lucky. Some of it isn't even recycled if your city water supply comes from a river downstream of another city using the river as a sewage dump.

48. How did you drink?

A water dispenser similar to a water gun was used to take a drink of water by holding the nozzle, or point of the dispenser, in the mouth and squirting the water directly in. Flavored drinks like coffee, tea, or orange were prepared by forcing water from hot or cold water dispensers into the plastic container. It held a flavored mixture which was dissolved by the water—we usually shook it to mix it. The plastic container squeezed up like an accordion and had a valve on the nozzle to keep the liquid from leaking out. To drink, we put the nozzle in our mouths, opened the valve with our teeth, and squeezed the bag to squirt the drink into our mouths.

49. Did you have trouble swallowing?

No. We had no trouble swallowing, but there was one bad aspect of swallowing drinks from the plastic drink containers. I think it bothered me more than the others. When I drank from the plastic squeeze-drink bags, I tended to swallow a lot of air with the liquid. This caused an uncomfortable pressure in my stomach which normally would be relieved by burping or belching. But—in weightlessness—the contents of the stomach don't settle; they coat the stomach more or less uniformly. So, if you burp, you stand a very good chance of regurgitating. The gas pressure in the stomach is unpleasant, but the consequences of burping are even worse. I think I only burped twice in eighty-four days. Once my exercise period had been scheduled right after breakfast and I had only been pedaling the bicycle a short time when I got this strong desire to burp. I fought it, but it happened anyway. I gritted my teeth, swallowed it, and kept right on pedaling.

50. How did you wash dishes?

Because we ate directly from plastic bags or cans, the only things that required cleaning were our tableware and food trays. These were wiped with tissues soaked with a mild disinfectant. The cans were crushed flat with a special food-can crusher and placed in a bag for disposal. We didn't throw anything into space.

WHAT DID YOU DO WITH THE TRASH?

51. What did you do with it (trash)?

Skylab had a large tank (2,000 cubic feet) which was used as a trash disposal volume. We compacted our garbage as much as possible, placed it in a special bag, and forced it through a large tube into the special tank below the floor. The tube contained an airlock chamber to prevent loss of air when we opened the hatch to the tube. The assembly was called a trash airlock.

The lid on the trash airlock began to cause difficulties on the second Skylab mission. The hatch became more and more difficult to latch in the closed position. On our mission, the problem became worse, and we were very concerned, because it was essential to get rid of the biodegradable garbage and waste (food residue and urine bags). We finally worked out a system whereby Jerry Carr would load the trash bag in the bin of the trash airlock and I would float above, holding onto the ceiling. As he closed the hatch, I would pull myself down sharply and stomp on the hatch lid while Jerry closed the locking lever. It sounds like a barnyard procedure, but it worked.

52. How did you wash dirty clothes?

We didn't. When they got dirty, we threw them away. All waste was put into the large waste compartment at the rear of the space system. (See Question 51.)

WHEN CLOTHES GOT DIRTY, WE THREW THEM AWAY

53. What kind of underwear did you wear?

We wore standard manufactured briefs and T-shirts.

54. Did you use space pajamas? How did you get dressed, put on your socks and shoes?

We slept in our underwear. After we "weighed" ourselves each morning, we slipped on the Skylab T-shirts and trousers, and then floated into our shoes, which were left attached to the floor during the night. Because it was difficult to bend forward, we pulled our legs up to put on our socks and tie our shoes.

55. What would happen if your glove came off your space suit during a space walk?

All the air would have leaked out and the astronaut would have died.

56. How did you keep from getting too hot or too cold on a space walk?

We wore water-cooled long johns. Cool water was circulated through plastic tubing in this garment to remove body heat. We could control the water flow rate to keep us from getting too hot or too cold.

57. Did you wear glasses?

Yes. I took two pairs with me. I'm farsighted and needed glasses to read small print and indicators. I didn't wear glasses while in the space suit.

58. Can—may—astronauts wear contact lenses?

NASA does not have a written policy regarding contact lenses. However there appears to be an unwritten policy against using contact lenses in flight. To date (March 1985) contact lenses have only been used as a part of an eye experiment (Shuttle flight number eight).

59. Did you just float around when you slept?

No. One member of our crew tried this once, but it didn't work too well because he kept bumping into things. We slept in sleeping bags supported by a tubular metal frame that was strapped to the wall of the sleep compartment. We slipped into the sleeping bag feet-first through the neck holes. There were arm slits in the bag, so we could reach out. It had straps on the front and back that we could tighten to hold us in a steady, snug position, and there were extra sleeping bag wraps that could be zipped on for greater warmth. Airflow, light, and temperature could be controlled in each sleep compartment.

60. How long did you sleep?

About six hours was all we needed because we weren't using a lot of physical energy performing our tasks in weightlessness.

61. Was your sleep restful, the same as here on Earth?

Yes, but I think there is a difference. Tests made on Skylab showed that there is a change in the time you spend at the different levels of sleep. Also, many astronauts have been bothered by a peculiar effect known as "head nod." During full relaxation in sleep, the head develops a nodding motion. This nodding motion is thought to occur as a result of blood pulsing through the large arteries in the neck. Some astronauts have been awakened by nausea symptoms which they blamed on the head nod. Others have noticed the head nod, but did not feel any ill effects.

62. Did you snore? Did anyone snore on Skylab? Did snoring bother you or keep you awake?

No. As far as I know, no one snored on Skylab. In weightlessness, the position of the soft palate in the upper throat doesn't change with the body position, which is probably the reason people don't snore in space. Most snoring occurs when a person lies on his back, thus causing the soft palate to hang down and vibrate during breathing.

63. Did you have to do exercises?

Yes. Since it doesn't take much physical effort to move around in space, an astronaut must exercise regularly to prevent the muscles from getting weak. We were given about one-and-a-half hours a day to exercise.

I normally spent half an hour on the stationary bicycle, fifteen minutes using spring and pulley (reel-type) exercisers, and ten minutes walking on the treadmill. On our day off, we sometimes skipped all exercises except the treadmill. We usually listened to music, using a stereo headset, while we were exercising on the bicycle, to help pass the time.

One time I was playing a new tape in Joe Kerwin's selection and really pumping hard as the work load increased at the end of the workout. I was tiring fast and wondering if I would be able to finish when the overture from *William Tell* started. It really gave me a shot of energy and I finished with power to spare. I was really surprised how much the music affected my performance.

64. What happens to the sweat?

We got a lot of sweat on our backs when we pedaled the bicycle. It didn't drop off like it does here on Earth. The sweat on the back collected in a large puddle. By the end of half an hour of exercise, the puddle was as large as a dinner plate and about a quarter of an inch deep. It just sort of slithered around on our backs as we pedaled the bicycle. When we were done, we had to move very carefully to avoid slinging off a large glob of sweat. It would have stuck to the walls of the spacecraft or onto equipment and caused problems. We used an old towel to mop the sweat off our backs before bathing.

65. How did you keep from floating around while exercising?

Our shoes locked into the pedals of the bicycle, but this didn't take care of the entire problem. We needed something to hold our bodies down because we tended to float off the seat. We finally held our heads against a makeshift pad mounted against the ceiling to balance the up-force caused by pushing down on the pedals. For the spring and pulley exercisers, we locked our shoes in the floor to hold us in position while we exercised. The treadmill had a harness that held us down against the walking surface.

66. How did you go to the bathroom?

On Skylab, for the first time in space, we had a separate room for a toilet. It was called the Waste Management Compartment. A funnel-shaped device was used to collect the urine. Air was drawn through the funnel to make sure the urine was pulled into the collection bag inside the device. This bag was changed daily. A commode, or potty, was used for solid waste collection. It was mounted on the wall (remember, there is no up or down in space) and was lined with a porous bag that was replaced after each use. Air was drawn through the bag to settle the waste.

The bag containing the solid waste was removed after each use and dried in a heat/vacuum chamber. All solid waste was dried, stored, and returned to Earth for medical analysis. Also, each day a small sample of urine was taken and frozen. It, too, was stored and brought back for analysis.

The toilet seat was made of a plastic-coated, stiff cushion material. A seat belt had to be used to keep the user's bottom from floating off the seat. Proper use of the toilet was essential if one wanted to avoid losing friends.

Because of their recessed plumbing, women have a special problem urinating hygienically in weightlessness. To solve this problem, NASA studied the issue in detail. This involved the photography of the urination function performed by a group of women volunteers. Based on their data, NASA developed a unisex toilet which is used on the Shuttle. The unisex toilet consists of a potty seat similar to the Skylab commode, together with a urine collection device located near the front of the toilet seat.

In older spacecraft not furnished with a special toilet, the provisions were much cruder. Liquid waste was collected by the same method used on space walks (see next question). The urine was stored in a collector.

Solid waste collection was much more difficult. We used a fecal collection bag, about eight inches across, with an adhesive ring surface around the top. The user stuck this bag to his bottom. After use, the solid waste

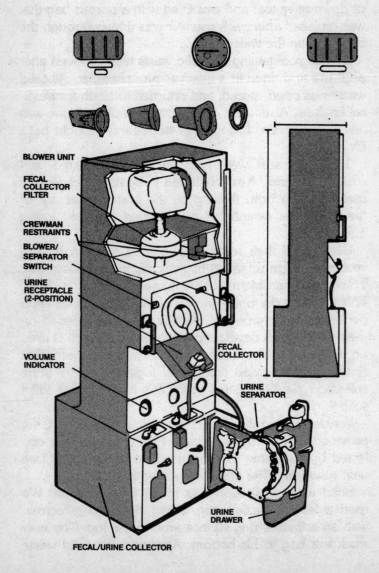

BLOWER UNIT

FECAL COLLECTOR FILTER

CREWMAN RESTRAINTS

BLOWER/ SEPARATOR SWITCH

URINE RECEPTACLE (2-POSITION)

VOLUME INDICATOR

FECAL COLLECTOR

URINE SEPARATOR

URINE DRAWER

FECAL/URINE COLLECTOR

was treated with chemical tablets to kill bacteria, and the bag was placed in a waste container.

This technique wasn't foolproof. Occasionally, fecal matter inadvertently floated free, unobserved by the user, and later drifted in view. Usually, no one would admit responsibility, and the event was cause for a lot of ribald comments. I can personally attest that fecal and urine spills can break the monotony on even the dullest days in space.

67. How did you go to the bathroom on a space walk?

We had two devices to wear under our space suits. One was for collecting urine, and one was for containing solid waste. The urine bag was attached to an undergarment with Velcro and connected to the penis by a rubber sleeve containing a check valve to prevent urine from leaking back out of the bag.

For solid waste, we wore a thick pair of tight-fitting, thigh-length trousers called the Fecal Containment System. If required, the astronaut would go to the bathroom directly into this garment. I know of no one who ever used this system, but it was good that we had it available because we spent several hours out on space walks during Skylab. When we returned from space walks, we removed the waste collection devices and transferred the contents to the appropriate containers.

Male astronauts still use the system described above. Female astronauts use a garment similar to normal feminine underwear called a Disposable Absorbent Containment Trunk (DACT). The DACT is lined with a one-way transmission layer that conducts liquid waste to a superabsorbent material that is capable of holding over a quart of liquid. The DACT is also worn during ascent (boost) and reentry by female crew members.

68. How did you bathe?

We had to bathe just about every day because we got very sweaty during exercise. On work days, we took a sponge bath, using a washcloth, soap, and water; on our days off, once a week, we had about a half a gallon (two liters) of warm water for a shower.

To take a sponge bath, we started by gently squirting water on a washcloth from the water dispenser in the bathroom. The water stuck to the washcloth and looked like a thick layer of gelatin; we had to move it carefully over to our bodies. As the water touched the body, it would stick and spread over an area a bit larger than the washcloth. The entire body was wetted this way, then lathered with soap. Then, as much soap lather as possible was removed with the washcloth, which could be wrung out in a special cloth squeezer. Next, water was again spread on the body and again mopped up, until the soap was removed. A towel was then used to dry. It took about thirty minutes to take a sponge bath.

A shower also took a long time—about half an hour. We had a zero gravity shower stall, which was a circular sleeve, about three feet in diameter, with a stationary bottom attached to the floor and a circular top mounted on the ceiling. The sleeve's wall surface was fastened to the top when ready to shower and fully enclosed the user. Once inside the shower stall, a spray nozzle was used to squirt water on the body and a vacuum cleaner attachment was used to suck off the soapy water both from the skin and from the walls of the shower stall. It was important to save enough water for rinsing off the soap.

I really did not enjoy the shower. It took a lot of work to get the equipment set up and I got chilled after the shower. The air was so dry that when I opened the shower stall, the rapid evaporation caused uncontrollable shivering for about a minute.

69. How did you shave?

We had commercial twin-blade razors, brushless shave cream in a tube, and also a wind-up rotary mechanical razor. I tried the wind-up razor but found it to be very poor. It pulled. I shaved with the blade razors for about two weeks, then stopped shaving and grew a beard. The blade razors were only good for one smooth shave, probably because there was no good way to rinse the shaving cream and whiskers from under the blades. We wiped the razor off on a washcloth and then rinsed the washcloth by squirting water on it and wringing the cloth in a special washcloth wringer. It took about fifteen minutes to shave; so, when I stopped shaving, it freed up some valuable early morning time.

70. Did you age less on your space journey? How much?

According to the theory of relativity, time passes more slowly for: (a) a person in a higher gravitational field than he normally experiences. (b) a person under accelerated motion, or (c) a person traveling at very high speeds (near the speed of light). For example, a person on the first floor of a tall office building ages more slowly than a person on the top floor (the difference is extremely small), because the gravitational attraction is stronger on the lower floor. Similarly, an astronaut experiences several minutes of accelerated motion during the launch and reentry phases, thus the aging is slowed. However, once in orbit, the aging rate is higher, due to the lower gravitational field. I don't know what the final result is, but I think the increased rate of aging in orbit exceeds the effect of the decreased rate during accelerated flight. In any case, the difference in aging is extremely small.

71. Can you hear as well in space?

We had difficulty hearing each other beyond twenty-five feet. Part of this was due to the noise level in Skylab, but some of it was probably caused by the thin air, as the atmosphere was about one-third as dense as air on the Earth's surface. There was no detectable change in the ear's ability to hear. The Space Shuttle cabin pressure is about the same as on the Earth's surface.

WE HAD DIFFICULTY HEARING
EACH OTHER

72. Did you have trouble talking? Did your voice change at all?

No, we didn't have any difficulty talking, even though the air was much thinner than air on Earth. We did not notice any change in voice pitch like the "Donald Duck" effect that deep-sea divers notice from breathing a thin or low density gas such as helium.

73. Do things taste and smell the same?

There are some slight changes in the sense of taste and smell. On our flight, we repeated taste and odor tests that we had done on Earth before the flight. The results were different for each person, and no consistent patterns were determined.

74. How did you tell time?

We wore commercial wristwatches and also had several clocks in the spacecraft. Our daily routine (work/sleep times) was based on Central time in the United States. Of course, day and night periods in orbit changed much faster than on Earth. We had sixteen sunrises and sunsets every twenty-four hour Earth day.

75. How can you tell up from down?

In weightlessness, there is no up or down insofar as your body feel is concerned. However, we did prefer moving to a position so that things "looked" right-side-up to the eyes. It was amusing to watch one of the other crewmen looking out the window toward Earth. He would always move his head or body around until his head was "up" facing the horizon.

76. Does it make you dizzy when you do tumbling and acrobatics?

Yes, in a way. Doing rapid rotations or tumbling gives you a strong giddy, dizzy feeling like you get on a ride at an amusement park. The strange thing about it is that the dizziness isn't disorienting or the least bit nauseating. It's a fairly powerful sensation with no ill effects. We still don't quite understand it.

77. What is a space suit made of?

A space suit may have as many as fifteen layers of material. Starting from the inside, a space suit contains the following materials:

1. A soft comfort layer of heat-resistant material called Nomex;
2. A gastight bladder of cloth-reinforced rubberlike material, neoprene-coated nylon;
3. Many layers of insulating materials;

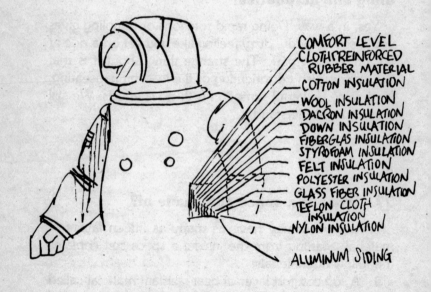

COMFORT LEVEL
CLOTH REINFORCED
RUBBER MATERIAL
COTTON INSULATION
WOOL INSULATION
DACRON INSULATION
DOWN INSULATION
FIBERGLAS INSULATION
STYROFOAM INSULATION
FELT INSULATION
POLYESTER INSULATION
GLASS FIBER INSULATION
TEFLON CLOTH
INSULATION
NYLON INSULATION

ALUMINUM SIDING

A SPACESUIT MAY HAVE
15 LAYERS

4. A protective outer layer of glass fiber and teflon cloth to protect against small meteoroids and fire.

The bubble helmet is formed of a high-strength plastic called Lexan. Altogether, it weighs about forty pounds.

78. What did you do for entertainment?

We had an entertainment kit which included books, playing cards, squeeze-type hand exercisers, some balls, a Velcro-covered dart board with Velcro-tipped darts, three stereo tape players with headsets and cabinet speakers, and a pair of binoculars. We each selected our own music tapes and books in advance of our mission, and these were sent up in Skylab when it was put into orbit.

We used the tape players, binoculars, and books more than any of the other items. The darts didn't work too well. Their fins were small, and because of the thin atmosphere in Skylab (one-third the atmospheric pressure of Earth), they wobbled around when they were thrown. The second Skylab crew tried enlarging the fins, but it didn't help much.

Sometimes entertainment opportunities came up quite unexpectedly. We had dry-roasted peanuts in small cans with thin plastic covers. The covers had crisscross cuts to allow us to reach in with our fingers to pull out the peanuts. Occasionally, a peanut would float out of its container, and as we made our way through the space station, we would notice it drifting and tumbling through the air. When this happened, we would get against the wall, open our mouths wide, shove-off toward the peanut, and try to capture it with our mouths like a fish. Some-

THERE IS NO UP OR DOWN

times we were lucky enough to catch it on the first attempt, but usually we would bump it, which would send it twirling off away from us.

79. What was your favorite entertainment?

I found that looking at the Earth with the binoculars was the most pleasant form of off-duty activity. The Earth was fascinating, and I never tired of looking at it. Next to this, I enjoyed the books and music the most. Floating acrobatics were also a lot of fun.

80. Did you have any puzzles?

No, but I think that's a great idea. I enjoy working crossword puzzles and cryptograms. In the future, I think electronic games will be used on space missions. They could be designed to improve operator skills in performing certain experiments on board.

81. Could you play basketball in space?

We didn't, but that's an interesting possibility. I don't think you could play basketball in the normal way. Dribbling would be a real challenge. We had three small balls in the recreation kit, and we played with them occasionally. When we threw them around, they bounced

THEY BOUNCED ALL OVER THE PLACE

all over the place because of weightlessness. The hardest part was trying to find the ball when you were done. I do think it would be possible to think up an interesting ball-and-hoop game for weightlessness.

82. Were you excited or scared at liftoff?

One of the NASA doctors asked me this same question, and I told him I didn't feel particularly excited. He said, "Well, that may be true, but your heart rate went from 48 to 120 at liftoff." I still don't think I was scared, but I must have been excited.

83. What was it like on the rocket going up?

When the engines fire up, they sound like muffled explosions, and there are a lot of noises from engine pumps and liquid fuel (propellants) surging through the large pipes (feed lines). Early in the launch, there is a lot of shaking and vibration. As the rocket picks up speed, it lurches, twitches, and wiggles from thrust pulsations and abrupt swiveling (gimbaling) of the engines to steer the rocket. It feels like being on top of a long weenie that's being shoved through the sky. There is a lot of swishing air noise as the rocket picks up speed. After the speed becomes supersonic, the swishing air noise and the engine roar suddenly stop, and then you can hear the noises from deep within the rocket, mostly creaks and groans. When the fuel is burned out of the first stage, it is discarded or cut loose by explosives (pyrotechnics).

This is really an experience—it sounds like a train wreck. There are banging noises and flashes from the explosives and from the little rocket engines that pull the spent stage away from the tail of the next stage. You can also see a lot of metal pieces flying away and twirling lazily around the rocket. Staging only takes a few seconds, but it seems much longer. Then the engine of the next stage fires, and you're off toward orbit.

84. Were you ever really scared?

An old cliché often quoted by pilots is that "flying consists of hours and hours of boredom interrupted occasionally by moments of stark terror." I've also heard test pilots and astronauts say that they don't experience fear, merely varying levels of anxiety or apprehension. I think some of them are telling the truth, but I also think they are expressing a distinction between fear and panic. A person can be genuinely afraid but, through discipline, self-control, training, experience, and professional competence, can still function rationally and effectively to cope with problems or emergencies. It is also true that a person can become conditioned to react with some degree of detachment when faced with serious and life-threatening situations, particularly when they occur within the individual's area of professional expertise. If anyone can claim such self-control, I think it would be experimental test pilots, particularly those that are still around to talk about it. However, I believe anyone is capable of experiencing fear—and a high level of concern for personal safety, prestige, or professional status. The key is to avoid panic at all costs, and this is best achieved by being well trained. Also, I don't equate excitement with fear. A bit of controlled excitement really gets the mind alert and working.

85. What is the greatest fear in space?

The greatest concerns are fire and the loss of air from the spacecraft. We had fire extinguishers on Skylab, and we also had emergency procedures to follow in the event of fire or rapid loss of pressure.

One day the fire alarm sounded as I was exercising on the bicycle. It was a blood-chilling sound, and I never liked to hear it, even when we were testing the alarm system. It turned out to be a false alarm, but it took me about half an hour to check out everything.

86. Did you get homesick?

I didn't get homesick in the strictest sense, that is, I didn't fret about it. We all missed familiar faces, but it wasn't a real psychological or emotional problem because we were so busy. We were also mentally prepared to stay in space for eighty-four days; that was our goal, and we were psychologically oriented to the eighty-four day mission.

There was also an interesting personal reaction I observed in myself as we neared the end of the eighty-four day mission. There was some consideration of extending our mission for two more weeks. We didn't hear too much about it on board, but we were unanimously opposed when some veiled suggestions were made. We quickly pointed out that we were out of food, which was technically correct. However, we probably could have used contingency food and scraped together enough spare meals to last two weeks. I remember thinking that extending the mission was a lousy idea. I had stayed up for the agreed-upon time, and that was that. In retrospect, I think my reaction would have been different if the approach had been different and had been made by the right person or if some emergency or operational problem had required it.

We all missed being around people, particularly family and friends. When we got back, it was very satisfying just to have a lot of different faces around.

87. What was the hardest thing to get used to?

The head congestion or stuffiness. This was a minor problem on most space flights, but I seemed to have it a bit worse than my two fellow crew members. In space the sinuses don't drain as readily as they do on Earth; there's no post-nasal drip in space.

88. Didn't you get bored on such a long mission of eighty-four days?

We were kept very busy, so boredom wasn't a problem. I would have really enjoyed having had more time to relax and look out the window at the Earth.

WE COULD HAVE SCRAPED TOGETHER
ENOUGH SPARE MEALS

89. Was it possible to get any privacy?

Yes, we each had a separate sleep compartment with a fabric door and we would use this to read as well as sleep. Also, Skylab was quite large, so it was possible to get privacy by going to another part of the space station.

One rather amusing aspect of our sleep compartments was caused by the Velcro strips that latched our doors, which were really fabric sheets, on the sleep compartments. When one of us got up at night to go to the bathroom, we opened the door by pushing open the Velcro strip. It sounded like someone was ripping open a shipping crate, and it frequently awakened the others. One night Jerry woke me, so I got up to look out the window for a few minutes. He was already there; we were over the Pacific Ocean somewhere and finally figured out we were flying over the Society Islands. We saw Tahiti, but it was mostly under clouds. After watching the coast of Chile come up, we gave it up and went back to bed.

90. How did your crew get along together?

Just fine. We were usually very busy, and there were so many problems with equipment that we had to help each other often. We had a good team spirit.

91. Did you ever get mad at each other or have fights or arguments?

We didn't have any fights, and there was only one argument that I can recall. It had to do with a change in procedure, and the instructions were very vague. We resolved this by trying the procedure to see if it worked. We never got truly angry at each other, but we were frequently upset with or had disagreements with some people in Mission Control. We were all trying hard to get a job done, so there was probably fault on both sides at one time or another.

I think I upset Ed Gibson one day by putting his ice cream in the food warmer and leaving his steak in the freezer. I really felt badly about it. He couldn't eat the steak because it was still frozen hard, and the ice cream had turned to milk. He had to dig out some contingency food to eat. There wasn't too much conversation at dinner that night. He salvaged the ice cream by refreezing it. In liquid form it had turned into a big hollow ball. The next day, after it refroze, he stuffed it full of freeze-dried strawberries and had the first strawberry sundae in space.

92. Are you all still friends?

Yes.

93. What would you do if another guy went crazy?

This is not a silly question. Isolation and confinement can cause severe mental stress in some people, and it's difficult to predict to whom it will occur and also the extent of irrational behavior. Our crew had talked with an individual who had witnessed one such derangement in an Arctic situation, and he gave us a good idea of the warning signs. There are a lot of symptoms well before the time a person might cause harm to himself or others. The first sign is surliness and a general tendency to be uncooperative; the next is withdrawal from others. After a period of reclusiveness, the person gradually becomes openly antagonistic and aggressive toward others. If I were to have this problem, I would expect the other crewmen to use whatever means available, be it medication or physical force, to control me while preparing to make an emergency/precautionary deorbit and return to Earth.

94. Did anyone get sick and vomit?

Yes. I threw up the first day of the flight. This was an unpleasant surprise because, according to tests we took while preparing for our mission, I was the least likely one of our crew to get sick. I used a vomitus bag similar to those available on airlines.

About one-half of the astronauts feel sick the first few days in space, but after about three days this is no longer a problem.

WHAT IF ANOTHER GUY
WENT CRAZY?

95. Were you prepared to take care of medical problems?

Yes. We had been given limited medical and dental training.

We had been trained to treat broken bones and sew up cuts. Also, we could talk to doctors on the Earth to get advice. We could have even showed the doctors the problems by using television which we could send down to Earth.

We could cope with non-serious problems, but in the case of serious injury or illness, we would have given the person emergency treatment and returned to Earth. For example, if a person had an appendicitis attack, we would have given antibiotics to control infection and brought him back at the first good opportunity. We had a heart needle and tracheotome to treat urgent emergencies like cardiac arrest and throat blockage.

We had a small pharmacy that included decongestants for stuffiness, sleeping pills, motion sickness pills, antibiotics for internal infections, and aspirin for headaches.

96. How did you know what medicine to use?

We used our own experience for minor things such as headaches and stuffy heads. For more complicated illnesses, we would have referred to our medical treatment book or consulted with the doctors on Earth.

WE HAD MEDICAL AND DENTAL TRAINING

97. What would you do if someone got a toothache?

First, we would have treated it with medication. If that didn't work, we had all the equipment and training necessary to remove the tooth.

98. If you cut yourself, would you bleed?

Yes, you would, but the blood wouldn't drop off.
It would collect in a ball over the cut. If there was enough blood, it would just spread out on your skin. We had tissues and bandages to clean and dress any wounds.

99. Did your position of sleeping, up or down, affect the body fluid shift?

No. There is no up or down in weightlessness, as far as the body is concerned. The fluid shift we experienced was caused by muscle tension in the legs which caused certain body fluids to move toward the head and upper body. It had nothing to do with our position.

100. What happens when you sneeze? Would it propel you backward?

I don't remember sneezing when I was free to float in reaction to the sneeze. In principle, it could cause a slight rotation backward and/or perhaps a slight upward movement. This is an intriguing question; I wish I had a few minutes back in space to explore the effects of a sneeze.

101. What could you see? What Earth features show up best?

Most of the time we saw oceans and clouds, but on almost every orbit we were able to get a good view of some land areas. The Earth features easiest to identify were coastlines, large lakes and rivers, major mountain ranges, and desert regions. Often it was like looking at a map, particularly when looking straight down at cloud-free land surfaces.

When we looked straight down toward the Earth, we could see a distinctive feature as small as a football field. Color or shading contrast and unusual shapes were particularly helpful in improving our ability to detect and identify features. We were able to see icebergs about a hundred yards in diameter quite easily because of the contrast of white ice with the dark blue sea.

When we looked at pieces of hardware in space, we were able to see them with much greater clarity because of the absence of air. We noticed this first during launch, when our escape rocket and spacecraft launch cover were jettisoned about fifty miles above the Earth. As the rocket engines pulled the cover off the front and away from our spacecraft, we were able to see an unusual amount of detail in the structure of the cover. It seemed as though we could see every rivet and join-line in it. When we got into orbit and turned around to look at

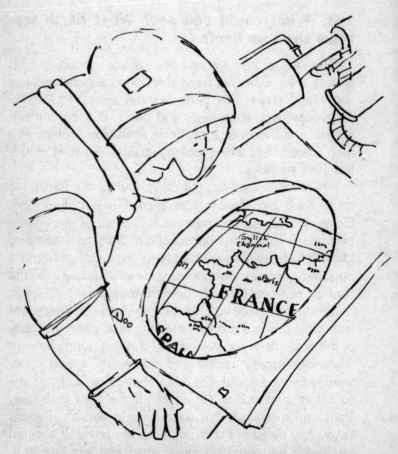

IT WAS LIKE LOOKING AT A MAP

our booster and, later, when we closed in during rendez-vous with Skylab, we noticed the same thing—an un-usual ability to see minute detail. In fact, objects looked so crisply and sharply defined that we got the impression we were looking at a finely drawn animation display. It was almost unreal.

102. Could you see . . . the Great Wall of China?

Yes, but we had to use binoculars. It wasn't visible to the unaided eye. The first time I thought I had seen it, I was in error; it was the Grand Canal near Peking. Later, I was able to identify the faint line of the wall, which zigzags in a peculiar pattern across hundreds of miles.

. . . the Pyramids?

No. I was unable to see them even with the binoculars.

. . . lightning?

Yes. It was most spectacular in the equatorial regions where thunderstorms covered thousands of square miles. We could also see lightning in thunderstorms on the horizon over fifteen hundred miles in the distance.

. . . the Grand Canyon?

Yes. It was very easy to see and identify. The colors of the walls of the canyon were quite obvious. After snowfall had covered the northern and southern rims, the colors were most vivid.

. . . the Golden Gate Bridge?

No. We could see San Francisco Bay, but I was unable to see the bridge, even though I knew where it was.

. . . the Aswan Dam of Egypt?

Yes. It's quite large and stands out clearly against the desert terrain. The Nile River is also very easy to see for the same reason.

. . . the "airfields" of ancient astronauts, as popularized in books and television programs?

No. We examined the Plains of Nazca, at the foot of the Peruvian Andes near the Pacific coast of South America, but were unable to see the patterns in the plains. I took several pictures of this area and there are some very faint patterns—squares with circles inside. This is not similar to any of the patterns shown in aerial photographs of the area.

. . . lights at night?

Yes. In industrialized countries the lights are not only visible but are quite bright. Cities and major highways are very easy to see at night. (See Question 103.)

. . . the aurora: northern and southern lights?

Yes. The aurora was the only Earth feature in which I could detect motion. The aurora patterns are variable and appear as dusky yellow tubes, spikes, sheets, and sprays.

103. I've read that visitors from another world, observing the Earth from several hundred miles up, would see no evidence of man's presence. What could you see that would indicate the presence of an advanced civilization?

I believe that statement was originally made after the first pictures of Mars showed no evidence of past or present civilizations, like canals or roads or structures. I think the features we saw that gave the clearest evidence of man's presence on Earth were the lighted cities and highways at night. It is a most impressive sight, and I think they could be seen from great distances out from the Earth. It would be interesting to observe the night side of the Earth from the moon during an Earth eclipse of the moon. This would shield the sun and permit you to look at the full night side of the Earth. I believe it would be possible to recognize North America or Western Europe under favorable weather conditions.

Other features that might reveal the presence of man, depending on the distance of the observer, would be aircraft contrails, crop and range land patterns, the Suez Canal, reservoirs in desert areas, large airfields, and (alas!) smog pockets.

104. Is the Earth prettier from space?

On a Skylab space walk, we could see about sixteen hundred miles to the horizon and had a much wider field of view than when looking through a window from the inside of the spacecraft. We had a good view of about 200,000 square miles (within 45° of vertical) of the Earth's surface and a clear and unrestricted view of the night sky. The view of the Earth was enthralling, if not downright soul-stirring. Once, when I had just finished passing film out to Jerry Carr who was removing and replacing film in the solar telescopes, I looked down and noticed we were directly above Lake Michigan. I could see the city of Chicago quite clearly because of the cross-hatch pattern created by snow melt on the streets. I looked over to my left and saw the mountains of Montana on the horizon; to my right were the Appalachian Mountains—the scene was breathtaking.

The view of the Earth was so enticing that I unintentionally caused a problem with the control system of Skylab while I was out on a space walk Christmas Day, 1973. Jerry Carr and I had completed the film magazine retrieval/replacement for the solar telescopes and Jerry had begun a one-man task of repairing a solar telescope filter wheel mechanism. The repair job was taking a long time because the problem wasn't quite as simple as originally thought. I was stationed at a location where the view wasn't too good, so I decided to move to the end of the telescope mount where I could see better. It had a good set of foot restraints, and when we stepped into them, the body pointed out from Skylab with the head in a good position to scan the Earth. The view wasn't good; it was spectacular. I was really having a ball. By leaning around, it was possible to get a view of the entire horizon. It was truly like being on top of the world, and the scene was magnificent. I leaned back and looked over my head, as Jerry had done a few minutes earlier, and got the feeling of falling he had described. It wasn't a scary feeling, but somewhat like drifting lazily upside-down and watching the world roll by.

My supreme delight, however, was shattered by comments from Ed from the inside of the Skylab. He was making comments about problems, half talking to himself and half expressing exasperation with the control system of Skylab. I could tell from his comments that the large gyroscopes were acting up. One of the three had failed while Ed and I were out on a previous space walk and we were having trouble making the two remaining gyros handle the load. Ed was busily engaged with special computer procedures to keep the Skylab from going out of control. He had been so busy that he was only half-aware of my comments regarding the exquisite view from the end of the telescope mount. Suddenly, his scientific mind put it all together and he yelled at me to get back to my "hole" (work station). Just as suddenly, I also realized the problem and I was very embarrassed because I was the cause of it. The air that circulated through my space suit flowed out through an exhaust port on a unit in front of the suit. The escaping air had the same effect as a small rocket engine and was tending to roll the entire eighty-ton space station. I returned quickly to my work station to eliminate the problem and felt a bit undignified about the whole situation. One minute I was on the top of the world and the next I felt as meek as a kid caught with his hand in the cookie jar.

In the meantime, Jerry was having trouble reaching far enough to work on the telescope, so I moved down to help him. I ended up holding him by his legs and shoving him head-first into an area where he could reach the telescope and complete his work.

By the time we finished our work we had been out on the space walk for seven hours. It was my last space walk and certainly had been one of the most interesting sightseeing experiences of my life.

105. What does the Earth look like?

Astronauts in Earth orbit were 100–750 miles above the Earth, and although they could see the Earth's curvature on the horizon, the Earth looked similar to the view seen from high-altitude aircraft. Of course, the area in sight was much greater and features appeared smaller because of the distance. Although the oceans are uniformly blue, the land surfaces differ quite a lot in color, texture, and relief; both are often covered by large tracts of clouds. Cleared range lands and cultivated agricultural regions are among the most prominent man-made features visible from Earth orbit. In particular, the slight differences in color, soil texture, stage of growth, and use of fertilizers make the boundaries between fields quite apparent. Airfields with concrete runways, large reservoirs in arid regions, and lights at night are also easy to see. Major mountain ranges have a ribbed and ridged appearance and high peaks are snow-covered. Deserts and arid regions are prominent, distinctive, often very colorful, and usually cloud-free. They also have individual coloration and surface patterns that make them easy to distinguish. Tropical rain forests of equatorial regions are huge expanses of monotonous, mottled dark green; late in the day they are frequently covered with enormous thunderstorms that extend for hundreds of miles.

The view has an air of fantasy about it, and you grope for words to describe what you see. My personal reaction was one of feeling humble, awed, and privileged to be witness to such a scene.

106. What color is the Earth? What colors do you see?

The colors on land vary. Mountains in non-desert regions are usually a nondescript dark brown or charcoal; high peaks and slopes are often snow-covered. Some appear coal black, like the Black Hills of South Dakota and the interior ranges of northwestern China. Some desert mountains are reddish brown. Forests are dark, almost black, except in the equatorial rain forests of Brazil and Africa, where they appear a mottled dark green. Field crops and range lands are also dark green but lighter than the forests. New growth of field crops and grasses are a brighter green than maturing crops. The only bright green vegetation I saw was on small tropical islands.

Coral reefs and shallows were a beautiful shade of blue-green. Many lakes are light blue or blue-green from algae growth. The Great Salt Lake in Utah is crossed by a rail line causeway which divides it into two separate bodies of water, one red and one green. The color difference is caused by different algae and marine organisms which have adapted to different conditions present in the separated lake. Although the ocean, in general, is dark blue, ocean currents may appear green from marine organisms that are carried by the current. Occasionally large patches of red—Red Tides—appear within the green. When this happens, it creates beautiful swirl patterns of green and red in the solid blue mass of the ocean. The Falkland Current off the coast of Argentina is an iridescent bright pea-green.

The sands of the Sahara and Arabian deserts have the most beautiful colors on the surface of the Earth. From space, these deserts look like a beautiful abstract sand painting. It is a pattern of mixed textures and varying shades of black, brown, tan, red, maroon, and orange. Much of the interior of Australia is a rusty brown color which is uniform over wide areas. We found Australia very easy to recognize after a week in orbit and referred to it as the "Red Continent."

107. Can you see the moon, stars, and planets any better? Are they any brighter?

The moon, planets, and stars are a bit clearer and noticeably brighter, but you really can't see them much better than from the Earth's surface. We could see about 20% more stars than we could from the Earth's surface.

On my first space walk, I tried to identify constellations while I was on the night side of the Earth. At first, I was confused because I was unable to recognize familiar patterns. Although I realized I was seeing more stars than I was accustomed to seeing, it still took a few minutes before I was able to adapt to the new patterns and recognize major star groups. As you might expect, stars don't twinkle when viewed from space as the twinkle is caused by atmospheric interference.

108. Could you see some of the planets?

Yes. We were able to see Venus, Mars, and Jupiter.

109. What does a sunrise look like from space?

A sunrise or sunset seen from Skylab occurred about sixteen times as fast as one observed from Earth due to the eastward velocity of the spacecraft. The sunrise starts as a rosy glow in the atmospheric layers on the horizon. The glow brightens and spreads outward as the red deepens and the various bands of the atmosphere brighten in white, blue, orange, and yellow. Just before the sun breaks, a bright golden-yellow blooms and shoots across the bands closest to the horizon. As the sun rises, the brilliance is dazzling and it is necessary to look away. The Earth below also changes rapidly as dawn breaks. Long shadows from hills, mountains, and clouds create eerie shading patterns for hundreds of miles. On Skylab

16 SUNRISES EACH DAY

there were sixteen sunrises and sunsets in each day's twenty-four hour period.

Moonrise is also intriguing. The full moon's rise is rapid, like a sunrise. As it comes above the horizon, it appears flattened and similar to moonrise seen from Earth. However, the rising occurs so fast it looks like a bubble of air rising in water. As the moon climbs higher above the horizon, it appears to "pop" from a flattened ball into a full circle.

110. Are you always in light (darkness)?

When in orbit around the Earth, moon, or another planet, the spacecraft is in darkness when on the night side (the side away from the sun) and in light on the day side (the side facing the sun). On the way to the moon or another planet, or in very high orbit above the Earth, the spacecraft would always be in light. Of course, as you travel farther away from the sun, the amount of light received from it becomes less and less. If you traveled to Pluto, the planet farthest from the sun, the sun would only look like a very bright star.

111. How hot (cold) is it in space?

When on a space walk in orbit or on the moon, the temperature is 250°F in the sunlight and 250° below zero in the complete shade (on the night side of the Earth).

112. A Russian cosmonaut said he went into space and didn't see God. Did you see God in space?

I don't think anyone sees God in the literal sense. We have inner reactions to many evidences of God—the physical order of the universe, beauty, kindness, and love. In this respect, God is evident everywhere and is no more visible in space than on Earth. It would be a remote and rarely accessible God if we had to go into space to see Him. The magnificence of the view of Earth and the heavens as seen from space are truly awe-inspiring—the perception of God in such a situation is a personal feeling. I did feel I was seeing, or feeling, a new aspect of God.

113. What is a solar flare like?

It's seen as a sudden brightening of a small area on the surface of the sun. It is something like a violent thunderstorm on Earth, and it usually results in a sudden increase in radiation and particles that stream out from the sun. This increased emission can be a danger to space travelers in deep space—for example, astronauts on lunar missions or on the way to Mars.

114. What would the astronauts on deep space missions do if a solar flare happened?

Moon missions were fairly short, about eight to ten days, and the only protection for the astronauts was the spacecraft walls. In the case of a flare, they would have stayed in their command module and canceled their lunar landing, or they would have cut short their stay on the moon and returned to their command module. It provided more protection than the thinner walls of the lunar landing spacecraft. For long spaceflights, like a trip to Mars, the likelihood of being exposed to radiation is much greater, and special rooms or chambers would probably be provided to protect the crew following solar flares.

115. What did it look like when you looked into space?

The view of space from the sunlit side of the Earth is different from the view on the night side. On the day side of the orbit, space appears as a solid background of black. The sun, moon, and brighter stars and planets are visible, but the general impression is that space is a black emptiness. On the night side of the Earth, stars appear bright and sharp, but it seems that space is even blacker than on the day side—a vast void of outer darkness.

The effect of the night side view of space is most dramatic when out on a space walk. I got my first unrestricted view of the entire night sky just as I had stopped working on a jammed radar antenna. Dr. Gibson and I had given up trying to use a small flashlight to continue our work in the dark. I raised the visor on my helmet cover and looked out to try to identify constellations.

As I looked out into space, I was overwhelmed by the darkness. I felt the flesh crawl on my back and the hair

OVERWHELMED BY THE DARKNESS

rise on my neck. I was reminded of a passage in the Bible that speaks of the "horror of great darkness." Ed and I pondered the view in silence for a few moments, and then we both made comments totally inadequate to describe the profound effect the scene had made on both of us. "Boy! That's what I call dark."

116. Did you have any strange encounters?

No, but once Ed Gibson and I thought we were. We were on a space walk and had been working over an hour, attempting to repair a piece of equipment covered by an aluminum-coated plastic blanket. The repair work took about four hours, and we could only work when we were on the day side of the Earth, where Earth shine lighted the work area. I had been tearing off pieces of the blanket that covered an electronic box in order to remove and replace it. I had just gotten the box exposed when we noticed we were entering twilight, so we stopped working to wait for sunrise. The Earth below was in total darkness, but we were still in faint twilight because of our altitude. I had begun looking into the night sky to continue a star field study, when Ed said in a rather querying tone: "Look over there; are those UFOs? There are hundreds of them." I looked and saw a cloud of metallic purple and violet sparkling objects. The sky was black behind them and they glistened with unusual sharpness and clarity. We became rather excited as we described them to Jerry Carr on the inside of Skylab. He turned down the lights inside and looked out the window, trying to see what new and wonderful discovery we had made. We all laughed as we realized what they were.

HUNDREDS OF U.F.O.s

The shreds of aluminum-coated plastic I had torn off had been blown away by the exhaust air from our space suits and had created a huge cloud of tiny reflectors several hundred yards out from Skylab. In the fading twilight of space they had popped into view and created a dazzling, twinkling cloud to decorate the night sky. They were still visible in twilight several hours later, after we had finished our space walk and reentered the Skylab. It was Thanksgiving Day, and while we had our turkey that evening, we were able to look out the window and see the twinkling tinsel of our unintentional Christmas decorations.

117. Do you believe there is other intelligent life in the universe?

No, or I should say I'm not convinced. It seems reasonable to believe there is other intelligent life, but "believing" does not make it so. Based upon our limited understanding of the universe and life forms, there exists the distinct possibility that intelligent life exists elsewhere in our own or other galaxies. To change this possibility into fact requires for me some form of undisputed scientific evidence, not mere conjecture or statistical guesswork. At present, such evidence does not exist.

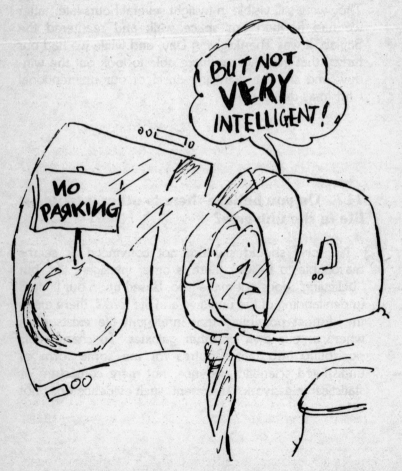

OTHER INTELLIGENT LIFE

118. What about the UFOs that accompanied our spaceships to the moon? (Astronauts have been quoted as observing mysterious objects following them on the way to the moon.)

I think the reports of astronaut sightings were misconstrued. We often observed clouds of ice crystals that formed from water and urine dumps. I know of no unexplained well-defined material objects that accompanied our spacecraft to the moon. One such report turned out to be the third stage of the Saturn booster rocket.

119. Have NASA computers been used to verify events in the Bible? (A report was circulated in the early 1970s claiming that NASA computers analyses had verified the Biblical account of Joshua's commanding the sun to stand still—because of missing time in a computerized reconstruction of Earth time history.)

No. This report is entirely false.

120. Did the astronauts find evidence that others had been to the moon at some previous time? (There have been rumors that the astronauts found evidence of extraterrestrial life on the moon.)

If such evidence had been found, it would have been freely and widely publicized as a major triumph of space exploration.

121. Did we really go to the moon? I've heard that space exploration is all a hoax and is staged out in the desert for television transmission.

Yes, we went to the moon. Walter Cronkite wouldn't have lied to you.

122. What would happen if you looked at the sun?

Looking directly at the sun for even a moment can cause permanent injury to the eyes whether you're on Earth or in space. Don't ever do it. We had a gold coating on our helmet visors to protect us from ultraviolet rays from the sun. This coating also reduced glare and acted like sunglasses, but it still was not enough protection to permit looking directly at the sun. On one of my space walks, I had great difficulty attempting to photograph a comet near the sun. I was supposed to aim the camera by eye and eventually was able to sight the camera and keep the sun out of my line-of-sight by getting into a position where the disc of the sun was blocked out and shaded by one of the large solar arrays.

123. Did you have a special instrument for looking at the Earth? the moon? planets? stars?

We had many instruments for the scientific study of the Earth. These included cameras and instruments that sensed various types of radiation from the Earth's surface. One of these instruments included a viewing telescope used to guide a sensing device that detected radiation from a very small area on the Earth's surface. Small features studied by this instrument included volcano craters, unusual desert areas, lake and reservoir surfaces, forests, meadows, and coppermine waste piles. We used this instrument to look at the moon, but only for evaluating the instrument itself. I used two instruments to make navigational sightings on the moon, stars, and the Earth's horizon, but they weren't for viewing as such. They were designed to see if a person could take manual readings accurately enough to determine spacecraft position and altitude in reference to the Earth.

124. Did you miss sex?

Yes, the thought did occur to me from time to time.

125. Could you have sex in weightlessness?

Love will find a way.

126. Could you smoke in space?

It probably would be possible to smoke, but it would be dangerous because of the fire hazard and undesirable because of the air pollution. I don't smoke, but some astronauts do. Most of them quit smoking several weeks before they went into space. I know of no difficulty the smokers had while they were in space. After return, virtually all resumed smoking.

127. If you could smoke in space, what would happen to the smoke and the ashes from a cigarette?

The smoke would contaminate the air temporarily, but would be eventually removed by charcoal air filters. The ashes could possibly drift around and get in the eyes or be inhaled and cause irritation. It isn't the most pleasant habit to accommodate in space. Smoke (or warm air) rises on Earth because it weighs less than colder air—in space everything is weightless, so there is no force to cause the circulation we normally observe around a candleflame or bonfire. If there were no air circulation from fans, the smoke would hover in a cloud around the smoker—a just and appropriate situation.

128. How big was Skylab?

It was about one hundred feet long and weighed eighty tons. The space inside was about the same as a three-bedroom house (12,500 feet).

SMOKE WOULD HOVER
AROUND THE SMOKER

Skylab was launched by a modified moon rocket (Saturn V), which was as tall as a thirty-three story building (330 feet) and weighed a little over six million pounds.

129. How long did it take to build Skylab?

About six years.

130. What did Skylab cost?

Skylab cost $2.6 billion over a seven-year development period.

131. How much did your space suit cost?

About $400,000.

132. What kind of spacecraft did you use to go up to Skylab?

We went up to Skylab in a special Apollo-type command and service module. The command module separated from the service module just before reentry.

A SPACESUIT COSTS $400,000

Overall, it was about the size of a travel-trailer (35 feet long, 12.8 feet in diameter) and weighed 30,000 pounds. The cabin volume—the space inside the command module for the astronauts—was about the same as the inside of a station wagon.

The command module was shaped like a cone. The conical shape was similar to the shapes of the earlier Mercury and Gemini spacecraft. The heat shield covered the curved base of the cone. The overall shape was adopted because the designers had experience with it and were confident it could accomplish reentry following the return from the moon as well as reentry from Earth orbit.

133. What was the heat shield made of?

On Mercury, Gemini, and Apollo spacecraft, it was made of a silicon compound chemically similar to sand. These heat shields actually burned away or flaked off (ablated) during reentry.

The maximum heat shield temperature was 5200°F during Earth orbit reentry and approximately 8000°F during lunar return reentry.

134. After reentry, how much did the chutes slow down the command module? How fast were you dropping on the parachute at splash-down?

The parachutes opened at ten thousand feet above the ocean and slowed our descent to about twenty miles per hour at splashdown (about thirty feet per second).

135. How big was the rocket that launched you into orbit?

The Saturn IB was about 225 feet tall and weighed 1,300,000 pounds.

136. What kind of metal was your spaceship made of?

Most of the metal in the structure of spacecraft and rockets is aluminum. Where high strength is needed, steel, titanium, and other alloys or composite materials may be used.

137. How many pieces are in the rocket (spacecraft, Skylab)?

The large Saturn V moon rocket had hundreds of thousands of parts in the three major sections (stages). The Apollo command module had over 2,000,000 parts; Skylab had about 150,000 parts.

138. How many people work for NASA?

Approximately 21,380 (as of January 1985).

139. How fast did you go?

We traveled at a speed of 17,500 mph (about five miles per second) while on Skylab, at an altitude of 270 miles (415 km) above the Earth's surface.

We circled the Earth over 1,200 times during the eighty-four days we were in space, which adds up to 34,500,000 miles.

140. Did you hit any meteoroids? What would happen if you did hit one?

Yes, but all were very small, the size of a tiny speck of dust. We had special test surfaces mounted outside on Skylab which were called micro-meteoroid samplers. Tiny meteoroid particles made miniature craters when they hit some of the samplers. A meteoroid larger than a pin head (1/16 inch diameter or larger) would probably burn a hole in the wall of a spacecraft. Assuming no one was hit by the tiny fragments, the worst problem arising from the hole would be a loss of air. The larger the meteoroid, the worse the problem. The hazard from meteoroids is actually very small.

WE TRAVELLED AT 17,500 MPH
(5 MILES PER SECOND)

141. How did you generate electricity?

On Skylab, large surfaces called solar arrays were covered with small devices (solar cells) which converted sunlight into electricity. Part of the electricity generated on the sunlit side of the Earth was stored in batteries for use on the night side. The command module used fuel cells which combined oxygen and hydrogen to generate electricity and water. The Space Shuttle also uses fuel cells.

A fuel cell is a device that combines two chemicals to produce electricity. Spacecraft fuel cells combine oxygen and hydrogen gases to produce electricity and drinking water. A fuel cell is like a cheese sandwich, with two porous metal plates (the slices of bread) on each side and a chemical (the cheese) in between. Oxygen is forced in through one plate and hydrogen through the opposite plate. The oxygen and hydrogen gases combine on the inside of the sandwich to form water. The water is removed as it is formed and piped to the drinking water supply. During this chemical process, a flow of electrons occurs between the plates to create a capability to deliver electricity to the spacecraft power system. The chemical (cheese) in the sandwich is a strong alkaline solution. Spacecraft fuel cells currently in use employ potassium hydroxide as the chemical filler for the fuel cell sandwich.

142. How did you heat the spacecraft?

When required, electrical heaters warmed air that was circulated through Skylab. Most of the time, though, the need was to cool the spacecraft, because a lot of heat was produced by electrical and electronic equipment as well as by sunlight on the sides of the spacecraft.

143. What kind of lights did you have?

On Skylab we had over eighty light fixtures that used fluorescent bulbs.

144. Did you grow any plants on Skylab?

Dr. Gibson grew rice plants on our mission. The purpose was to determine the growth rate and direction of stem growth in weightlessness. A light was shone on the plants continually, in an attempt to make the stems grow straight toward the light, but they sort of turned and twisted as they grew. It really looked strange.

145. Did you use plants to control the amount of carbon dioxide expired by crewmen?

On Skylab, we did not use plants to remove carbon dioxide, but this may be possible in the future. This technique may be used on long space missions to other planets, on a permanent moon base, or in a space colony.

146. How did you control the carbon dioxide level in the spaceship atmosphere? How could you tell what it was?

On Skylab, we used a device called a molecular sieve to trap and remove carbon dioxide exhaled by crewmen. Air was forced through the sieve, a device manufactured by pressing metal powder into a cake or solid block. The spaces between the powdered metal particles were large enough to let nitrogen and oxygen pass through, but not the large molecule of carbon dioxide. We had an instrument to tell us the concentration level of carbon dioxide in the air.

Our command module used a different system. A chemical, lithium hydroxide, was used to absorb the carbon dioxide. The Space Shuttle also uses this method.

147. How much radiation exposure did you get?

I got a total of forty rems, which is about twelve hundred times what I would have received on the Earth's surface during the same eighty-four day period. This was about one-quarter the maximum allowable dose. I received most of it while outside Skylab on space walks.

The radiation was measured by personal dosimeters, also called film badges, that were carried on our clothing and space suits. There were also two other instruments used from time to time for measuring radiation levels at special locations inside Skylab.

148. Where does space begin?

Earth is really a part of space, but we tend to think in terms of "outer space" as beginning at some distance away from the Earth. We in the United States say that a person has been "in space" if he goes more than fifty miles above the Earth (approximately 265,000 feet). However, during reentry, the spacecraft actually starts to "feel" the Earth's atmosphere at about seventy-five miles above the surface of the Earth (about 400,000 feet). We call this altitude the "entry interface." There are all sorts of practical terms of reference for everyday flight-planning purposes. We might say that we enter outer space when nature's rules of orbits have much greater influence on the vehicle than do nature's rules of travel in the atmosphere.

149. What does it look like when you're going up?

As the rocket climbs vertically, the sky gradually turns from blue, to dark blue, then to dark violet, and finally to jet black. As the rocket gradually noses over to a level path, it is possible to see the Earth's horizon and the Earth. It is very surprising the first time you see the horizon because the layer of air, our Earth's atmosphere, looks so thin. I used to think of it as a thick blanket, but now I think of it as a thin sheet. If one could imagine an apple as big as the Earth, 99% of the atmosphere would be thinner than the skin of the apple.

WHERE DOES SPACE BEGIN?

150. What keeps you in orbit?

A British scientist named Newton gave a very good explanation of an orbit back in the seventeenth century. Suppose you are standing at the North Pole of the Earth and looking south toward Canada and the United States. Further, suppose you can throw a ball as fast as you desire and that air drag doesn't exist. First, you throw the ball and see it land in Hudson Bay, Canada. Not satisfied, you wind up and throw it faster and see it land in Lake Michigan. The third ball is even faster, and you see it land in the Gulf of Mexico. The fourth ball is faster yet and falls in Argentina. Finally, you really put your back into it and the ball doesn't even touch the surface of the Earth as it goes over the Antarctic and the South Pole. As you stand there considering what happened to the ball, it suddenly whizzes past your shoulder from behind you and streaks toward the south again. What happened is, you threw it hard enough to send it all the way around the Earth. In other words, you put it into orbit. It is actually falling, but it is going so fast that its path of fall is the same as the curvature of the Earth. If there were no air resistance and the Earth a uniform spherical mass, the ball would continue to "fall," or orbit, indefinitely. This is why a spacecraft can stay in orbit for a long time without running the engines. It is actually "falling" and is still being pulled by Earth's gravity, but its great speed keeps it from taking a path that would cause it to hit the Earth's surface.

The orbital lifetime of a satellite depends on several factors—its distance or altitude above the Earth (moon, planet, sun, etc.), the shape of the orbit, the density of the atmosphere, and, perhaps, the shape and density of the satellite. For example, the Earth is in orbit around the sun and it will remain in orbit around the sun for billions of years. A satellite in orbit above the Earth at an altitude of about one hundred miles will only stay in orbit for several months. Skylab was in orbit at an altitude of 270 miles and it stayed up for six years.

151. Don't the rocket engines pollute the atmosphere and space?

Many rockets use hydrocarbon- or petroleum-derived fuels in the first stage, and some pollutants are produced. The upper stages usually employ liquid hydrogen and liquid oxygen which are very clean, so very little pollution is caused in the Earth's upper atmosphere or in space. The attitude rockets and orbital maneuvering engines on the orbiting vehicle cause a small amount of pollution in the form of oxides of nitrogen.

152. How much pollution is caused by a launch?

For the Space Shuttle, many tons of aluminum oxide (AlO_2) and hydrochloric acid (HCl) are produced by the solid rockets. The liquid propellant engines in the Orbiter produce virtually no pollution. All rocket engines utilize combustible propellants and there are exhaust products. Some of the products are considered pollutants; others are not. For example, the exhaust products from hydrogen-oxygen used by the Shuttle's main engines are water, plus some free oxygen and hydrogen; the exhaust products from RP1 (kerosene) and LOX (liquid oxygen) used in the first stage of a Saturn rocket include carbon monoxide, carbon dioxide, water, carbon, and some unburned kerosene (hydrocarbons). The engines used in orbit to control attitude and make adjustments to the orbit and for deorbit use nitrogen tetroxide (N_2O_4) and monomethyl hydrazine (CH_3NHNH_2). The products of combustion of these propellants include oxides of nitrogen, carbon monoxide, carbon dioxide, ammonia, water, and free hydrogen, oxygen, and nitrogen.

153. What good is it to look down at the Earth? Give me one example of something you saw that did some good on Earth.

NOTE: This was not a hostile question; it was asked by a student to force me to explain the practical value of Earth observations—it turned out he wanted to become an astronaut.

I reported a branch of the New Zealand current near the Chatham Islands that was previously unknown to exist. This report was challenged by ground teams who thought I had made a mistake in reporting the location. I later verified it on a subsequent orbit and ships were dispatched by the Australian Navy. They confirmed my report. This was important because it was a new fishing area unknown. Currents carry plankton which is the base of the ocean food chain (the "bread of the sea"). Small organisms are eaten by larger ones and this process continues until commercial food fish are present.

Our crew was the first to receive formalized training to prepare us to make deliberate visual observations for specific purposes. Although our training was limited, it did give us a good idea of what information the scientists wanted. We observed the growth cycle of crops in Australia and Argentina, structural (geologic) fault lines in many areas, weather effects, and ocean surface phenomena, and we studied several desert and arid areas.

Based upon observations of the Sahel, a broad region spanning the continent of Africa south of the Sahara Desert, I theorized that enormous quantities of dust were being carried high into the atmosphere and far out to the sea. Six months later, automated satellites verified that dust clouds travel over vast distances. Satellite photos were used to observe the movement of a dust cloud from Africa all the way to the Caribbean sea.

Not only is observing the Earth an enjoyable aesthetic experience, but it also has immense practical value.

154. I read in a book that there were cracks in the interstage structure of the rocket that took you into space. Is this true?

Yes, there were "stress corrosion" cracks in the interstage trusses that connected the two stages of our Skylab-4 booster. These cracks could only be seen with a magnifying glass.

155. Wasn't this a bit risky?

The stress corrosion cracks weren't considered to be a serious problem and were only discovered during detailed inspection following replacement of cracked fins on our rocket. Our launch had been delayed a week for the fin replacement and when we were told about the stress corrosion cracks I remarked to Jerry Carr that we ought to name our booster rocket "Humpty Dumpty" because they were finding so many cracks in it. Later, Jerry casually mentioned our proposed name to the launch pad manager who had been working around the clock supervising the repair work crews who had accomplished the fin replacement and inspection work. He didn't appear to find the remark amusing.

The next morning we were atop the rocket in our spacecraft waiting for launch. In between the many checks we were confirming with the launch director, he would read "Good Luck" messages from the different teams that had participated in our training and launch preparation. It was rather nice and helped pass the time. Finally, the launch director said, "I have one final message," and Jerry Carr said, "Go ahead." The launch director read it slowly: "To the crew of Skylab 4, Good Luck and Godspeed—signed: All the King's horses and all the King's men." We had a good laugh and thanked the repair team for all their hard work. It somehow seemed reassuring to know they had a good sense of humor.

156. Did you have 100% oxygen in the space station?

No. Skylab had a mixture of 75% oxygen and 25% nitrogen at a total pressure of five pounds per square inch (about 35% sea-level pressure).

157. What was it like during reentry?

Our reentry began in darkness. Before we even felt the slowing effect of the atmosphere, the spacecraft became surrounded by a faint white "cloud." As the air friction increased, the white cloud changed to pink, then deepened to rose, and finally became a fiery mix of orange and red with streaks of bright red particles from the heat shield in the trail of hot gases behind the spacecraft. As the thrusters fired to roll the spacecraft for corrective maneuvers, the rocket plumes caused wild swirls in the hot gases, and the patterns of flame seemed to spiral crazily along the edges of the wake of fire. The whole thing lasted about four minutes, during which we were subjected to a peak force about four times our own weight. It was such a fascinating and beautiful display that I didn't even notice the build-up of heavy force on my body. Then it seemed like it was suddenly over, and we were falling down through 100,000 feet in a gradually steepening trajectory. The rest was just procedures—the real fun was over.

158. How do you stay cool and comfortable during reentry heating?

The heat shield is a very effective insulation material, so very little heat passes through to the inside. Even though the temperature may reach 8,000°F on the heat shield, the inside of the spacecraft remains comfortable.

159. What did it feel like when you entered gravity again?

Everything felt very heavy, including our own bodies. I picked up a three-pound camera just after splashdown and it felt like it weighed fifteen or twenty pounds. When I rolled over on my side in the spacecraft couch to pick up the camera, it felt like one side of my rib cage was collapsing onto the other. These exaggerated impressions of heft and weight only lasted a few days and, for the most part, disappeared completely in less than a week.

160. Did you have any difficulty adjusting to gravity again?

There were several incidents that I found disconcerting:

1. We were able to walk, but were a bit unsteady at first. I involuntarily turned to the right, even though I was looking straight ahead and trying to walk straight. I also drove off the right shoulder of the road twice during

WE LOST ALL OF THE HEIGHT

my first week back. It was as if I were watching someone else drive—a weird and confusing sensation. One passenger suggested that NASA was putting something in our Tang. Another remarked that this wasn't at all abnormal for a Goldwater man. I was a bit upset because I didn't understand what was happening, and after I drove off the road the second time, I was very careful. This "right turn" tendency went away after the first week. I didn't tell the doctors for fear that they might ground me or use me as a guinea pig for more medical tests. I haven't had any further problems with this since the first week following the flight.

2. Almost all of the astronauts have dropped things during the first few days after return. In weightlessness, they had become used to releasing objects and having them float nearby until needed again. This was a great convenience in performing even simple tasks. I dropped the toothpaste tube and I almost dropped a glass of water on the bathroom floor the first morning after return. I felt it slipping in my fingers and gripped it again just in time. This tendency also goes away in a few days.

3. Another problem I noticed was a tendency to fall or roll out of bed. The NASA doctors got smart fast on this one. The beds we used on the aircraft carrier that picked us up were fitted with side rails. I thought this was ridiculous when I saw it. I was wrong. I tried to "float" out of bed that night, and the rail saved me from a fall.

4. Heaviness in bed was another post-mission sensation. It felt like I was collapsing the bed when I lay down—as if I weighed several hundred pounds. The pressure distributed on my body from my weight seemed excessive for about four or five nights.

5. On the third night after my return, I struggled out of bed to go to the bathroom and I got lost in the dark. I was turning to the right again.

161. How long does it take to get back to normal?

After our eighty-four day flight, it took about five weeks for our bodies to return to our normal pre-mission physical condition. The Russians have said it takes a cosmonaut about seven weeks to recover fully from a six-month flight.

162. How many engines are on the Shuttle?

Fifty-one engines are used by the Space Shuttle vehicle:

1. Two solid rocket booster (SRB) engines, with 2,600,000 pounds thrust each, used during the first two minutes of launch;

2. Three Orbiter main engines, with 470,000 pounds thrust each (vacuum), for launch only;

3. Two orbital maneuvering system (OMS) engines, with 6,000 pounds thrust each, for orbit insertion, orbital maneuvers, and deorbit;

4. Thirty-eight primary reaction control system (RCS) engines, with 900 pounds thrust each, to control the Shuttle attitude in orbit and make small translations;

5. Six vernier (fine control) RCS engines, with 25 pounds thrust each, to make small adjustments in attitude.

163. What is the most people the Shuttle can carry?

It can carry a maximum of ten for rescue missions. Seating can be provided for a crew of three (rescue crew) and seven passengers (the crew being rescued).

164. How much does the Shuttle weigh at liftoff?

The Space Shuttle vehicle weighs approximately 4,400,000 pounds at liftoff. The Space Shuttle Orbiter, the reusable spacecraft, weighs from 200,000 to 250,000 pounds, depending on payload carried.

165. How much can the Shuttle carry into space?

The Shuttle can carry as much as 65,000 pounds to equatorial circular orbits up to 230 miles. Smaller payloads can be delivered to circular orbits up to 690 miles. The higher the orbit, the less payload that can be carried—because the extra weight of fuel (propellant) needed to go higher must be subtracted from the payload weight. Also, if the launch is aimed to carry the Shuttle over or near the Earth's polar regions, the payload capability will be reduced because the Earth's rotation doesn't contribute to the launch. (See Question 185.)

166. Why doesn't the Shuttle use a heat shield like the older spacecraft?

The old heat shields actually burned away during reentry; thus, they could only be used once. Because the Shuttle is designed to make many flights into space and back again to Earth, it would be very expensive to put on a new shield for each flight; so they designed a new surface made up of tiles called the Thermal Protection System (TPS) or Reusable Surface Insulation (RSI). On a few of the early Shuttle flights some of the tiles were shaken loose from the upper surface during the launch and boost phase. In these problem areas the tiles have been replaced by Advanced Flexible Reusable Surface Insulation (AFRSI), a heat-resistant fabric.

167. What are the tiles made of?

They're made of a silicon compound coated with a ceramic material that protects the tiles so they aren't damaged by reentry heating. They are designed to last the life of the Shuttle spacecraft or for one hundred reentries through the Earth's atmosphere. The AFRSI fabric is a quilted blanket of Nomex felt coated with a white silicon material.

168. How do the tiles work to dissipate or reject heat?

The tiles get rid of 95% of the reentry heat by radiation (rapidly emitting the heat generated by air friction). The remainder of the heat is slowly conducted into the tile, and some of this heat diffuses out to be re-radiated after landing. A very small amount, about one percent, actually reaches the metal skin of the Orbiter vehicle.

169. What would happen if a lot of them came off?

It could cause the loss of the Shuttle during reentry. As noted in Question 166, above, on several of the early Shuttle flights some tiles were lost on the upper surface near the tail. These were not in a critical area and the missing tiles caused no serious problems during reentry.

170. How hot do the tiles get during reentry?

Although designed to tolerate a peak temperature of 2800°F, the highest temperature thus far experienced has been 2280°F.

171. How long a runway does the Shuttle need?

The Shuttle can land on a 10,000 foot runway, but it is better if the runway is 15,000 feet long. Many large civilian and military airfields have 10,000 foot runways. Because the Shuttle does not have engines it can use during landing, the longer runway makes it easier for the pilot to plan his landing.

172. Can it land on any airfield the right size?

Yes, but only a few airfields have all the special radio equipment to help guide the Shuttle toward the airfield. As the Shuttle pilots get more experience, they will probably become skilled enough to land on airfields without this special radio equipment. However, this would probably not be done except in an emergency.

173. On the Shuttle, how high up can they still eject?

Up to 100,000 feet.

NOTE: Ejection seats were active (capable of being used) on the two-man test flights of the Space Shuttle *Columbia*—the first four Shuttle flights. The Orbiters *Challenger*, *Discovery* and *Atlantis* are not designed to have ejection seats. The ejection seats in the *Columbia* were removed during retrofit (overhaul) in 1984.

174. Will it be possible to rescue Shuttle astronauts if they can't get back from space? If there were an emergency, how soon could you send help?

At the present time (1985), rescue might be possible if circumstances were just right, i.e. if a Shuttle were in the late stages of preparation for launch when another Shuttle became stranded in space. Even then a rescue launch might take as long as a week. The crew in space can extend survival time while awaiting rescue by conserving oxygen and other consumables. Present estimates by NASA technicians are that the stranded crew can survive a week for each day's worth of oxygen budgeted for average flight activity. Oxygen is used to generate electricity in the fuel cells in addition to replenishing the living compartment atmosphere.

175. How fast is the Shuttle going when it lands?

About 220 miles per hour.

176. How far does it roll after landing?

It depends on the speed at touchdown and the amount of braking used. Using maximum braking, the Shuttle can stop in about one mile. However, the tires and brakes would have to be replaced after a maximum braking roll-out.

177. How long does it take for the wheels to come down when the Shuttle is landing?

About six to eight seconds. The landing gear is lowered just before touchdown.

178. How long do the tires last?

They are designed for five normal landings.

179. When the Shuttle is reentering, when does it start to fly like an airplane again?

The aerodynamic control surfaces on the wings begin to be effective at about 250,000 feet altitude and a speed of 26,000 feet per second.

NOTE: The rudder does not become fully effective until the spacecraft has descended to 80,000 feet altitude. From 80,000 feet down to landing the Shuttle is controlled entirely by the control surfaces.

180. Why do the Shuttle astronauts have to wait so long to get out after landing?

They have to turn off all of the systems of the Shuttle, and they must wait for ground crews to make sure no harmful or toxic gases or fumes are still present in the air around the Shuttle. This takes about thirty minutes to one hour.

181. What causes the toxic gases? Where do the fumes come from?

The toxic gases or fumes are produced in two devices: (1) a gas turbine used to run hydraulic pumps for powering engine gimbals (steering controls), flight controls, and wheel brakes; and (2) an evaporator device used to cool equipment as the Shuttle descends below 80,000 feet.

The gas turbine is powered by gas pressure created by decomposing hydrazine, a caustic chemical. The evaporator–cooler uses a mixture of ammonia and water, because the ammonia evaporates more readily. An invisible cloud of these gases surrounds the Space Shuttle after landing and must be blown away by special fans used by the ground crews.

182. What kind of things would we want to build in space?

In addition to a multipurpose space station planned for the 1990s, some of the structures being considered are:

1. Large communication antennas: eventually most phone and television links will be through space relay units.

2. Solar power stations: solar energy collectors and transmitters.

3. Manned laboratories.

4. Space processing factories.

5. Storage warehouses.

6. Large spacecraft assembly facilities—for future space missions to the moon or Mars, for example.

7. Refueling and repair depots.

8. Medical research facilities.

183. Why spend so much money on space exploration when we still have sickness and hunger on Earth?

Most of the untreated sickness and hunger arising from inadequate domestic production occurs in areas that have not developed broad-based science and technology capabilities. These areas, often called underdeveloped countries, depend on the nations with advanced capabilities to help them. If we arbitrarily abandon human inquiry or exploration in a given area (astronomy, mathematics, genetic studies, or space), we may, unwittingly, deprive ourselves of advancements that would contribute to the solution of parts of these problems such as food production and distribution or medical care and treatment. This doesn't mean that space exploration is going to provide answers to solve hunger and health problems, although many space program developments have already helped in both areas. It is essential to realize that if we ignore or curtail participation in a frontier discipline or arena, it has a stifling effect on research and development in many other areas. Incidentally, the amount spent on space exploration is probably less than popularly believed. The entire NASA budget is about 1½% of the Federal Budget, or a penny of each tax dollar. This is still a lot of money, about $6 billion, but less than the amount Americans spend on toys each year. I feel that it is money well spent. (See Question 184.)

184. Are our current goals in space different from the Russians? Are we working on different things than they are?

Yes. The Russians appear to have as their major immediate goal the achievement of permanent manned presence in space, first in Earth orbit and later near the moon. Their space stations will become progressively larger, with the capability to accommodate larger crews and longer stays in space. They appear to be thinking of permanent stations on the moon, and some Russian spokesmen have predicted a Soviet mission to Mars before the end of this century. The Russians are now launching five satellites for each U.S. satellite and have resumed the lead in the manned exploration of space. Their goal is to achieve preeminence in space and, in the process, to demonstrate the superiority of their political system.

Official American goals are less ambitious and are becoming restricted to work in Earth orbit. We are primarily working on improving the quality of instruments used to observe the Earth and to decrease the cost of carrying equipment into space. Scientific satellite programs, planned to continue studies of the solar system, have been largely abandoned because money is not available. It is sad, but true, that political leadership in the U.S. has never grasped the philosophical and historical importance of space exploration. The Apollo lunar landing program clearly demonstrated American superiority in manned space exploration—this lead was surrendered to the Russians in the 1970s. The American lead in planetary exploration is about to suffer a similar fate. Throughout history, the most successful societies have explored new worlds and their progress has been stimulated by new discoveries. Space exploration will continue. If we in America don't do it, then other nations will.

185. Why is the launch center located in Florida?

The Air Force selected Cape Canaveral for missile testing in the 1950s, and when NASA was formed in 1958, it relied on Air Force experience and facilities to assist in the launches of the early spacecraft. Mercury and Gemini orbital space missions were launched by Air Force boosters (rockets) originally designed for missiles. During the 1960s, NASA developed its own launch facilities on Cape Canaveral at the Kennedy Space Center. These facilities have evolved into a highly reliable launch base for manned and unmanned spacecraft.

The Air Force chose the Florida location because of several favorable features of the site:

1. The secluded location simplified security.

2. The site faced the Atlantic Ocean; rockets could be launched eastward over the ocean without risk to the general population.

3. Rail, highway, air, and water transportation were reasonably accessible.

4. The mild subtropical climate provided moderate weather for year-round operations.

5. A southerly location in the United States makes the best use of the "sling-shot" effect caused by the Earth's rotation. The eastward motion of the Earth's surface due to its rotation adds over 1,000 mph to the speed of a rocket launched in an easterly direction at the equator. This advantage decreases progressively as the launch site is moved north or south of the equator. Thus, a launch site in the southern part of the continental United States would be best. At Cape Canaveral, the eastward surface velocity is almost 900 mph, a distinct asset for orbital launches.

186. What are the medical spin-offs from the space program?

I don't know all of them. One of NASA's responsibilities is to see to it that discoveries made in space pro-

FLORIDA LOCATIONS HAVE FAVORABLE
FEATURES

gram research and operations are offered to others who might possibly have a need for it. For example, image processing techniques developed to clarify pictures of planets can also be used to improve the quality of X-ray photographs to make it easier for doctors to detect tiny hairline fractures that might have gone undetected before. A system used to heat the faceplate of helmets has also been used to keep burn victims warm, as they can't tolerate blankets, and to provide uniform warmth for premature babies in incubators. It would probably take a good book to explain them all.

187. What benefits have we gotten from the space program?

That's a bit like asking, "What benefits have we gotten from our schools, colleges, and universities?" There have been many practical benefits from the space programs. Computer design, electronic miniaturization, medical equipment, management techniques, weather observation, and international communications have all benefited from developments made in space exploration. However, I believe the most important are the subtle and intangible benefits that have occurred within the minds and spirits of people. Among these benefits are aroused curiosity, the intellectual stimulation that attends exploration, an appreciation of the importance of goals, the virtue of dedication, the necessity of commitment, and belief in one's ability to accomplish. The overall attitudes of people influence their aspirations and ability to attain. Awareness of the achievability of difficult goals has a strong influence on the objectives we set for ourselves. I believe the most beneficial legacy of the space program has been to elevate our expectation of ourselves.

APPENDIX A
SUMMARY OF
PHYSIOLOGICAL EFFECTS

1. WEIGHTLESSNESS: FLUID SHIFT—An abnormally high volume of blood and tissue fluid tends to concentrate in the upper part of the body.

EFFECT OR SYMPTOM

1.1 Giddy, light-headed feeling
1.2 Bug-eyed sensation
1.3 "Flush" feeling in face
1.4 Awareness of neck pulse; throbbing in head
1.5 Distended veins in forehead and neck
1.6 Hypersensitivity to head movements; excessive or exaggerated sensation of rotation caused by head movements (Note 1)
1.7 Moderate to severe headache
1.8 "Full" feeling in head
1.9 Head stuffiness; nasal, sinus or ear congestion
1.10 Facial edema: puffiness in face; bags under eyes
1.11 Early flight malaise—nausea, vomiting (Note 2)
1.12 Bloodshot eyes
1.13 Reduced visual accommodation; decrease in ability to focus on near objects (most significant effect in older crewmembers)
1.14 Reduced total blood volume; orthostatic intolerance
   * Prolonged cessation of red cell production with

133

eventual stabilized total red cell population
commensurate with the reduced blood volume
(long flights)
* Post flight anemia (long flights)
1.15   Decreased girth measurements of thighs and
calves of legs due to lowered volume of blood &
tissue fluids in the legs
1.16   Fluid infusion into internal organs (U.S. tissue tests
on Cosmos in 1129)

2. WEIGHTLESSNESS: VESTIBULAR SENSITIVITY
EFFECT OR SYMPTOM
2.1   Hypersensitivity to head movements; excessive or
exaggerated sensation of rotation caused by head
movements (Note 1)
2.2   Early flight malaise—nausea, vomiting (Note 2)

3. WEIGHTLESSNESS; TISSUE FLOAT—The tendency of
surface and internal body tissue to "float" or shift upward on the body, in relation to its position as normally
observed on Earth.

EFFECT OR SYMPTOM
3.1   Facial tissue rise; high cheekbone, Oriental
appearance. In combination with facial edema
(puffiness), 1.10, above, facial appearance is
altered. Most edema subsides after three-five days.
3.2   Internal organs shift upward, creating a "wasp
waist" appearance and, possibly, a reduced vital
capacity or inability to breathe as deeply as on
Earth.
3.3   Hair float (long hair)
3.4   Raised or elevated breasts (females)
3.5   Floating or raised genitalia (males)

4. WEIGHTLESSNESS; MUSCULO-SKELETAL EFFECTS—
Changes occur in the relaxed body posture; ability to as-
sume certain body positions is reduced; bone demineralization occurs during early exposure to weightlessness.

EFFECT OR SYMPTOM
4.1   Relaxed body posture is semi-erect, knees bent
slightly, upper back curled slightly forward, loss of
curvature in small of back; arms float upward at
chest height, shoulders rise up in a "shrug"
position.

4.2 Spinal lengthening and straightening causes increased body length (height). Approximately 2 inches.

4.3 Inability or difficulty in bending forward or in assuming a seated position; seat belt required to hold body seated in chair. Easier to bend forward after several weeks.

4.4 Bone mass loss or bone demineralization occurs during early weeks of flight (extent of loss varies with the individual). Soviet flight results on long missions indicate the bone mass loss stops after extended exposure to weightlessness.

4.5 Loss (atrophy) of muscle mass and tone in the large muscles of the legs. Partially arrested by exercise during flight. Rapid recovery after return. Main cause is inability to achieve the normal workload stress present on Earth. Contributes to decreased girth measurements of thighs and calves (see 1.15, above).

5. WEIGHTLESSNESS; MISCELLANEOUS EFFECTS—Temporary episodic or periodic effects experienced

EFFECT OR SYMPTOM

5.1 "Space crud"—a general malaise or "down" feeling that occurs 3–4 hours after eating; similar to onset of flu or a cold. Quickly relieved by eating

5.2 Reluctance to belch; risk of regurgitation; excessive flatus due to gas retention (gas retention problem may be less for Shuttle—cabin pressure is higher)

5.3 Lingering body odor may occur if crewmember is in an area where fan circulation is poor (no convective circulation)

5.4 Head congestion is relieved by exercise and, to some extent, by eating (see 1.9, above)

5.5 "Head nod" during sleep probably caused by carotid pulse; causes nausea in some crewmembers (10%)

5.6 During heavy exercise, auxiliary fan circulation may be required to prevent overheating; sweat accumulation can be a problem

5.7 Eyeglasses may tend to bob up and down or fly off during rapid head turns if ear pieces don't fit properly

5.8 "Inverse déjà vu"; surroundings appear unfamiliar when viewed from unusual perspective; immediately corrected by assuming a familiar body position relative to the physical environment

5.9   Persistent tendency to throw objects too high when tossing items (apparently allowing for non-existent gravity drop)

6. SPACE RADIATION: EFFECTS DUE TO IONIZING RADIATION

EFFECT OR SYMPTOM

6.1   Radiation tissue damage (extent unknown)

6.2   Light flashes "seen" by dark-adapted crew-members when passing through low spots or regions in the Earth's radiation belts, polar regions or while traveling through deep space beyond the Earth's trapped radiation zones. (Note 5)

7. SPACECRAFT ATMOSPHERE; EFFECTS DUE TO LOW PRESSURE, LOW HUMIDITY OR, POSSIBLY, DUE TO HIGH OXYGEN CONCENTRATIONS. (Note 6)

EFFECT OR SYMPTOM

7.1   Tissue drying; chapped hands and lips, dryness in the eyes (eye irritation or sensitivity)

7.2   Peculiar soft or puffy texture/feeling in the mouth, sometimes described as a "cotton fuzz" feeling. Effect has not been well documented.

8. EFFECTS ON BASIC SENSORY AND PHYSIOLOGICAL FUNCTIONS OR PERFORMANCE DUE TO THE SPACE OR SPACECRAFT ENVIRONMENT

EFFECT OR SYMPTOM

8.1   Slight changes in sense of taste and smell; statistical differences slight—pattern varies with individual

8.2   No detectable change in motor skills or coordination tasks

8.3   Slight changes in proportionate time spent at various levels of sleep. Also sleep requirement appears to be 1–2 hours less (per day) for crewmembers while in space

8.4   Enhanced clarity of vision of objects viewed in space vacuum. This increased ability to see with increased sharpness has led some to describe such views as "gemlike" or "unreal in clarity." Most probably due to absence of light scattering in vacuum.

8.5   Ability to see 10–20% more stars (see 8.4, above)

8.6 Reduced visual accommodation (see 1.13, above)—most significant in older crewmembers

8.7 Visual scene orientation prejudice; predisposition to view scenes as one is accustomed to seeing them (even though there is no sensed gravity vector). Crewmember will move to orient "eye plane" to achieve the preferred scene orientation

8.8 Ambient spacecraft noise can vary from benign to distracting levels and may affect a crewmember's ability to go to sleep

9. POSTFLIGHT REACTIONS

EFFECT OR SYMPTOM

9.1 Postflight anemia (see 1.14)

9.2 Perception of magnitude of heft and weight forces
* Objects feel heavier
* External body pressure sensations due to sitting, lying (particularly when rolling on one's side) feel unnaturally excessive

9.3 Muscle/tendon/joint soreness
* Lower back and calf muscle soreness
* Achilles tendon soreness/ache
* Knee joint soreness during long distance running

9.4 Standing/walking difficulties
* Faintness (orthostatic intolerance)
* Unsteadiness and balance problems

Note 1: Disagreement exists regarding the cause of hypersensitivity—whether it is a direct result of weightlessness, a secondary effect of the fluid shift or due to causes unidentified.

Note 2: Disagreement exists regarding the cause of early flight malaise (nausea)—whether it is caused by the fluid shift, hypersensitivity to head motions (a form of motion sickness), a combination of both, or due to an unidentified cause. American medical teams have insisted that the problem is due to a form of motion sickness and have attempted to treat it accordingly with a notable lack of success. Russian space personnel, reportedly, contend that the primary cause is the fluid shift; information is not available on the success of any preventive measures they have tried.

Note 3: Decrease in visual accommodation has been verified on Shuttle flights.

Note 4: General fatigue, slight nausea occasionally, degraded operator performance. "Space crud" was not noticed on long space walks (lasting up to seven hours).

Note 5: Three explanations have been proposed to explain the light flashes seen by crewmembers. A. Cerenkov radiation (emission of photons by particles slowed by fluid in the eye), B. Light generated by particles ionizing fluid in the eye, or C. Artificial light stimulus caused by particles impacting retinal sensors in the eye.

Note 6: Although the effects described in 7. above are more applicable to the low cabin pressures used in American spacecraft prior to the Shuttle, there may be times even on Shuttle missions when low cabin pressure will be used for operational reasons.

APPENDIX B
EARTH FEATURES
RECOGNIZABLE FROM SPACE

It is difficult to give a complete description of Earth features visible or recognizable from space. There are many variables to consider, such as: orbital altitude, season of the year, local time of day at the site being observed (sun overhead is best for most viewing), and, of course, individual differences among viewers themselves. However, because of the many questions on this topic, I have compiled a list of features that I thought were easy to identify from low Earth orbit (270 miles above the Earth's surface) during the third Skylab mission, November 16, 1973–February 8, 1974. It should be noted that, during this period, it was late fall and winter in the Northern Hemisphere and late spring and summer in the Southern Hemisphere. Other astronauts would have different opinions, so the listing should be considered opinionative. Still, it does give a fair idea of the types of things that can be seen and identified.

The features listed below are those that can be recognized at a glance. It is assumed that suitable weather and lighting conditions exist. Following many of the feature classification headings, I have enclosed in parenthesis the feature I considered to be easiest to identify in that classification.

139

A. Coastline Features

Coastline features are particularly easy to identify because of their unusual shape or outlines and the contrast between land and water.

1. Bays and Gulfs (Hudson Bay, Canada)
   San Francisco Bay, California; Gulf of St. Lawrence; Gulf of Venezuela; Arabian Gulf; Gulf of Oman, Oman; Gulf of Suez, Egypt; Gulf of Aqaba, Egypt; Gulf of Pohai, China; Galveston Bay, Texas; Mobile Bay, Alabama.

2. Major River Mouths (Rio de la Plata, Argentina/Uruguay)
   Amazon, Brazil.

3. Peninsulas (Valdes P., Argentina)
   Sinai P., Egypt; Kamchatka P., Russia; Korea; Italy; Crimean P., Russia; Baja California, Mexico; Florida; Gaspe P., Canada; Cornwall P., England; Antofagasta, Chile.

4. River Deltas (Nile Delta, Egypt)
   Ganges D., India; Irrawaddi D., Burma; Mississippi D., U.S. NOTE: The deltas of the Ganges and Irrawaddi look much alike, but the coastlines are different. The Mekong Delta was under clouds most of our flight.

5. Capes (Cape Cod, Massachusetts, U.S.)
   Cape Canaveral, U.S.; Cape Hatteras, U.S.; Cape Guardafui, Somalia.

6. Coastal Island Groups (Channel Islands, Catalina and San Clemente, California, U.S.)
   Florida Keys, U.S.; Long Island, N.Y., U.S.; Vancouver Island, B.C., Canada; island groups on the southwest coast of Chile; island groups on the west coast of Canada.

7. Straits (Gibraltar, Spain and Morocco)
   Juan de Fuca, B.C., Canada; S. Belle Isle, Canada; Dardanelles and Bosporous, Turkey; S. Magellan, Chile; Cook S., New Zealand.

8. Coastal Plains, Basins, Depressions (Los Angeles Basin, U.S.) Afar Triangle, Ethiopia; Namib Desert, S.W. Africa.

B. Ocean Features

1. Currents (Falkland Current, S. Atlantic off Argentina)

   NOTE: Currents may be visible due to plankton growth they carry. It is often a green (bright to dull) color and contrasts with the blue of the ocean. Red plankton growth may also be seen (Red Tides). There are undoubtedly seasonal variations in the color and conspicuousness of the currents. The Gulf Stream and Japanese Current were not readily visible. The Westwind Drift Current off the southern tip of Africa was visible, but not prominent.

   Brazil Current, Atlantic off Brazil; New Zealand Current, Southwest Pacific.

2. Islands and Major Island Groups (Japan)
   Taiwan; Malaysia and Indonesia; Sakhalin, Russia; Antilles, Caribbean; Hawaiian Islands; Britain and Ireland.

3. Coral Reefs and Shallows (Bahama Banks)
   Great Barrier Reef, Australia.

4. Temporary Ocean Features (Ice Islands, South Atlantic)
   Icebergs, sea ice (salt water ice); river silt and sediment; ship wakes.

C. Inland Geographic Features

1. Lakes and Seas (Great Lakes of U.S. and Canada)
   Great Salt Lake, Utah, U.S.; Lake Titicaca, Peru; Lake Popo, Bolivia; Lake Yellowstone, Wyoming, U.S.; Lake Victoria, Africa; Salton Sea, California, U.S.; Lake Powell, Arizona, U.S.; Lake Mead, Nevada, U.S.; Finger Lakes, N.Y., U.S.; Lake Maracaibo, Venezuela; Lake Baykal, Russia; Black Sea; Caspian Sea; Dead Sea, Israel/Jordan; plateau lakes of Tibet.

2. Dried Lake Beds (White Sands, New Mexico, U.S.)
Great Salt Lake Desert, Utah, U.S.; playas of the plateau
region of Bolivia; Rogers Lake, California, U.S.

3. Deserts (Sahara, North Africa)
Arabian D., Saudi Arabia; Mojave D., California, U.S.;
Gobi D., Mongolia; Great Desert region western Australia;
Kalahari and Namib Deserts of the southwestern Africa.

4. Mountain Ranges (Himalayas, Asia)
Alps, western Europe; Caucasus, Russia; Anticlines of Iran
(parallel system of hogbacks); Sierra/Cascade Range of
western U.S.; Sierra Madre Orientale, Mexico; New Zealand Alps; Front Range of Rockies, Colorado, U.S.; Black
Hills of South Dakota, U.S.; Appalachian Range of eastern
U.S.

5. Large Valleys/Basins (Grand Canyon, Arizona, U.S.)
Dead Sea Rift, Mideast; Rhine Valley (Basel to Strasbourg),
western Europe; San Joaquin V., California, U.S.

6. Plateau Regions (Tibet, Asia)
Andean Plateau, South America.

7. Miscellaneous Features Recognizable
   a. Glaciers
   b. Circular Impact Features
   c. Lava Flows
   d. River Flooding

D. Man-made Features

1. Reservoirs (Aswan, Egypt)

NOTE: Reservoir lakes are easy to recognize in arid or
desert areas or when contrasted with snow surrounding the
lake. Lakes in forested regions are much more difficult to
see.
Lakes Mead and Powell, Utah, Arizona.

2. Cultivated Field and Range land Boundaries
Seasonal variation in growth causes gradual changes in the contrast along field boundaries, but they are readily identified cultural features.

3. Cities (Los Angeles, California)
Mexico City; Buenos Aires, Argentina; Dallas-Ft. Worth, Texas; Houston, Texas; Denver, Colorado; Chicago, Illinois; New York City.
NOTE: Cities are not normally easy to see in the daytime, even though they are very easy to see at night. The single most significant feature that facilitates easy recognition is the pall of smog that accumulates over most all large cities. It is not confined to industrialized countries either. I never was able to see Addis Ababa, Ethiopia, because of the rather continuous layer of smoke and smog.

4. Miscellaneous Features Easy to See
   a. Aircraft Contrails (condensation trails)
   b. Smoke Plumes
   c. Fires at Night
   d. Large Airfields with Concrete Runways

E. Atmospheric Features

1. Clouds
Clouds of some form are almost always in view, but vary widely as to type. The most distinctive cloud features included the following:
   Tropical Storms: large spiral pattern
   Thunderstorms: hightops, anvil heads, lightning
      Cloud Wakes: alternating fish hook patterns down wind of islands and mountain ranges

2. Dust Storms (Sahara Desert)
Dust storms were visible variously as dense, well-defined bands; narrow, wispy streaks; and broad diffuse areas of dust suspended in air. The most peculiar dust storms were those in the Gobi Desert where snow mixed with the dust

created strange brown and white patterns. The areas where dust storms were most prevalent follow:
   North Africa (Mauritania to Egypt)
   Central Africa (Niger River Inland Delta)
   Australia (Great Deserts of central and western Australia)
   Gobi Desert of Mongolia

3. Miscellaneous
   a. Aurora Borealis
   b. Lightning
   c. Meteors
   d. Smoke, Smog, Haze
   e. Sunrise/Sunset Effects

APPENDIX C
GUIDE TO INFORMATION
& RESOURCES

1. General educational space-related materials—Educators, teachers and students:
Write, explaining your need or requirement, to the NASA Field Office serving your state (see Table 1, below) or to the NASA Headquarters address listed in the Table.

2. NASA Educational Publications Mailing List—for educators and teachers only:
Write to the address(es) in Table 1, providing the following information with your request to be placed on the mailing list.

> Your position/title (Name optional)
> Name of school or institution and mailing address
> Level of material: Elementary, Junior High, High School,
>   College or other (specify)
> Subject Interest:
>   Sciences: Life, Earth, Physical, Mathematics,
>   Astronomy, Aeronautics;
>   Other: Humanities or specify

3. Educational Kits, Learning Packets and Textbooks on Aerospace developed by the Civil Air Patrol. These materials are of

excellent quality; request catalogue brochure and price list from the Regional Director of Aerospace Education serving your area (see the listing in Table 2). Note: these Directors are available for providing other services in addition to educational materials. Teachers or educators may obtain advice and assistance in organizing courses, summer studies, obtaining speakers, etc.

4. Information and assistance in obtaining photographs, other than standard NASA lithographs.

To obtain *earth photographs or imagery* taken by aircraft, spacecraft or satellites, contact:

> User Services
> EROS Data Center
> Sioux Falls, SD 57198 Phone: 605/594-6522, ext 151

Explain the purpose of your order and ask for an order form which will contain the latest price list.

If you don't have a photo or image file number for the geographic area (or the specific photo you have in mind), you may be able to get help from the User Service office at the EROS Data Center (above) or from the Audio Visual Branch, Public Information Division Code, FP, NASA Headquarters, 400 Maryland Ave., S.W., Washington, DC 20546.

Note: NASA does not accept orders for photographic prints, negatives or transparencies. You may order prints as suggested above, or order negatives or transparencies from the offices listed and make your own prints. Raw space photographs and images are public domain and not subject to copyright restrictions, *BUT* a photo or image that has been enhanced or assembled into a mosaic by a private laboratory can be protected by copyright, and will so list its claim on the product.

5. Information and technical assistance for serious technical/ scientific research or for the practical applications of data and developments generated in NASA programs: The latter may include a variety of close assistance services for industry or small businesses even extending to the assignment of patents.

If you're not sure where to begin, start by contacting the Technology Utilization Officer at the NASA Field Office serving your area (Table 1).

For general advisory on photographic or imagery services for earth graphics contact User Services at the EROS Data Center (see 4., above).

For cartographic applications of space imagery contact:

> National Cartographic Information Center
> U.S. Geological Survey
> 507 National Center, Room 1C107
> Reston, VA 22092 Phone: 703/860-6045

For more specific applications for your business or activity contact the following:

> Director, Technology Transfer Division
> NASA Scientific and Technical Information Facility
> P.O. Box 8757
> Baltimore/Washington International Airport, MD 21240

The Director can refer you to a number of various offices that specialize in different areas of NASA Technology Utilization.

To obtain advisory guidance you may be able to get limited assistance from the following:

> Library of Congress
> National Referral Center, or the Congressional
> Research Service
> Washington, DC 20540
> Library of Congress Switchboard: 202/287-5000

> House Committee on Science and Technology
> House of Representatives
> Washington, DC 20515
> 202/225-5629 or 6275

TABLE 1

Residents of	write to: Public Affairs Office:
California (northern) Idaho Montana Oregon Washington Wyoming	NASA Ames Research Center Moffett Field, CA 94035 415/965-5543 or 5544
Arizona California (southern) Nevada Utah	NASA Jet Propulsion Laboratory 4800 Oak Grove Drive Pasadena, CA 91103 213/354-2423
Colorado Kansas Nebraska New Mexico North Dakota Oklahoma South Dakota Texas	NASA Johnson Spacecraft Center Houston, TX 77058 713/483-4241
Illinois Indiana Michigan Minnesota Ohio Wisconsin	NASA Lewis Research Center Cleveland, OH 44135 216/433-4000, Ext 444 or 708
Alabama Arkansas Iowa Louisiana Mississippi Missouri Tennessee	NASA Marshal Spaceflight Center MSFC, AL 35812 205/453-0038
Florida Georgia Puerto Rico Virgin Islands	NASA Kennedy Space Center KSC, FL 32899 306/867-4444

Kentucky North Carolina South Carolina Virginia West Virginia	NASA Langley Research Center Hampton, VA 23665 804/827-3966
Connecticut Delaware District of Columbia Maine Maryland Massachusetts New Hampshire New Jersey New York Pennsylvania Rhode Island Vermont	NASA Goddard Spaceflight Center Greenbelt, MD 20771 301/344-7207
Foreign countries *	NASA Headquarters Community Services and Educational Branch (LFG-9) Washington, DC 20546 202/755-0816, or 3756

Materials available from the above offices include brochures, booklets, lithographs of photos and illustrative art (including large posters for bulletin boards), films and audio tapes. Note: NASA films and audio tapes may be reproduced locally on recording devices for future use without copyright infringement.

For television urgent requirements, station should call: 202/755-3500.

* For films in foreign languages, contact USIS at the American Embassy in the national capital of your country.

TABLE 2

USAF-CIVIL AIR PATROL
REGIONAL DIRECTORS OF AEROSPACE
EDUCATION
May 1980

GREAT LAKES LIAISON REGION
(IL, IN, KY, MI, OH, WI)
    Mr. Phil Woodruff
    Director of Aerospace Education
    USAF-CAP Great Lakes Liaison Region (MCLGLR)
    Wright-Patterson AFB OH 45433
Ofc. Ph: (513) 257-6836

MIDDLE EAST LIAISON REGION
(DE, MD, DC, NC, SC, VA, WV)
    Mr. Walt Flint
    Director of Aerospace Education
    USAF-CAP Middle East Liaison Region
    Andrews AFB MD 20331
Ofc Ph: (301) 981-6229/5273

NORTH CENTRAL LIAISON REGION
(IA, KS, MN, MO, NE, ND, SD)
    Mr. Melvin A. Ziehl
    Director of Aerospace Education
    USAF-CAP North Central Liaison Region
    Bldg 751, Mpls-St Paul Intl Airport
    Minneapolis MN 55450
Ofc Ph: (612) 725-5361

NORTHEAST LIAISON REGION
(CT, MA, ME, NH, NJ, NY, PA, RI, VT)
    Mr. Robert C. Smith
    Director of Aerospace Education
    USAF-CAP Northeast Liaison Region
    Bldg 17–31
    McGuire AFB NJ 08641
Ofc Ph: (609) 724-2967/2931

PACIFIC LIAISON REGION
(AK, CA, HI, NV, OR, WA)
  Ms. Jule Zumwalt
  Director of Aerospace Education
  USAF-CAP Pacific Liaison Region
  Mather AFB CA 95655
Ofc Ph: (916) 364-2554

ROCKY MOUNTAIN LIAISON REGION
(CO, ID, MT, UT, WY)
  Mr. Noel A. Bullock
  Director of Aerospace Education
  USAF-CAP Rocky Mountain Liaison Region
  Lowry AFB CO 80230
Ofc Ph: (303) 370-3075/3082

SOUTHEAST LIAISON REGION
(AL, FL, GA, MS, PR, TN)
  Mr. Kenneth C. Perkins
  Director of Aerospace Education
  USAF-CAP Southwest Liaison Region
  Bldg 802
  Dobbins AFB GA 30060
Ofc Ph: (404) 429-5268/9

SOUTHWEST LIAISON REGION
(AZ, AR, LA, NM, OK, TX)
  Mr. C. E. Neal
  Director of Aerospace Education
  USAF-CAP Southwest Liaison Region
  USNAS
  Dallas TX 75211
Ofc Ph: (214) 264-2353

For special requests write: The Center for Aerospace
Educational Development, National Headquarters, Civil Air
Patrol, Maxwell AFB, Al 36112-5572. Phone (205) 293-5371.

PRINTED AIDS TO OBTAINING ACCESS TO RESOURCES

1. *NASA pamphlets and publications*
The following publications may be obtained from the NASA facility serving your area (see Table 1).

EDUCATION SERVICES: A one-piece folder explaining NASA educational services available to students, teachers, schools and community organizations.

NASA EDUCATIONAL PUBLICATIONS: A ten-page booklet listing current educational publications, curriculum resource materials, NASA fact sheets, classroom picture sets and scientific publications (updated frequently).

NASA FILMS: A thirty-page booklet listing films available for free loan (return postage and insurance required) to educational, civil, industrial, professional, youth and similar groups (updated periodically).

NASA PHOTOGRAPHIC INDEX: An index of representative photographs covering the various NASA programs. Instructions for ordering prints included.

SPINOFF: An annual publication (100 + pages) intended to promote the transfer of technology developed within the NASA programs to diverse elements of private business, industry and other local or national service agencies. Gives representative examples of contributions (spinoffs) of NASA-developed technology. Contains section describing the mechanism employed by NASA to achieve technology transfer and to assist other parties (private as well as governmental) interested in exploiting NASA-developed technology.

2. *Other Government publications:*

THE EROS DATA CENTER: A booklet explaining products and services (assistance) available through the EROS Data Center. Includes a good listing of information sources for those interested in learning more about earth resources studies possible with space graphic products. Order from: User Services EROS Data Center, Sioux Falls, SD 57198.

BIBLIOGRAPHY

1. Government Publications: May be ordered from Supt. of Documents, U.S. Govt. Printing Office, Washington, DC 20402.

The following official histories of the major American space programs document the human and technical effort required to achieve the success of each program. Exhaustive references are cited which should prove to be very helpful to anyone seeking to do historical research. Although voluminous and somewhat tedious at times, I would recommend that anyone aspiring to be an astronaut read all these books to appreciate fully all the disparate interests and considerations pertinent to the development of space programs.

Swenson, Loyd S., et al. *This New Ocean: A History of Project Mercury*, NASA SP-4201, NTIS, 1966*.

*Available from the National Technical Information Service Springfield, VA 22161 Phone: 703/557-4600

Hacker, Barton C., et al. *On the Shoulders of Titans: A History of Project Gemini*, NASA SP-4303, GPO, Washington, DC, 1976.

Brooks, Courtney G., et al. *Chariots for Apollo: A History of Manned Lunar Spacecraft*, NASA SP-4205, GPO, Washington, DC, 1979.

Compton, David W., et al. *Living and Working in Space: A History of Skylab*, NASA SP-4208, GPO, Washington, DC, 1983.

Ezell, Edward C. and Linda N., *The Partnership: A History of the Apollo-Soyuz Test Project*, NASA SP-4205, GPO, Washington, DC, 1978.

The following references have been prepared by researchers in the Congressional Research Service, Library of Congress. Aside from classified intelligence sources, they represent the best data available to the public on the topics covered.

Smith, Marcia, *Astronauts and Cosmonauts Biographical and Statistical Data*, GPO, Washington, DC, 1981.

Sheldon, Charles S., *Soviet Space Programs, 1966–1970*, GPO, Washington, DC, 1971.

Sheldon, Charles S., *Soviet Space Programs, 1971–1975*, GPO, Washington, DC, 1976.

Sheldon, Charles S., *Soviet Space Programs, 1976–1980*, GPO, Washington, DC, 1981.

Sheldon, Charles S., *United States and Soviet Progress in Space, Summary Data Through 1979 and a Forward Look*, GPO, Washington, DC, 1980.

The following are well-illustrated publications that outline the events within the programs discussed.

Cortright, Edgar M., *Apollo Expeditions to the Moon*, NASA SP-350, GPO, Washington, DC, 1975.

Belew, Leland F., *Skylab, Our First Space Station*, NASA SP-400, GPO, Washington, DC, 1977.

2. Commercial Publications:

Gatland, Kenneth, *The Illustrated Encyclopedia of Space Technology, A Comprehensive History of Space Exploration*, Crown Publishers, New York, 1981. (An excellent reference book, well-illustrated and useful for serious study as well as informative browsing. A valuable addition to the reference section of libraries.)

Oberg, James E., *Red Star in Orbit*, Random House, New York, 1981. (Highly readable and informative look at the Russian space program including discussions of several controversial topics related to Russian objectives, motives and conduct of space exploration and utilization.)